Praise for
SUCCESS—PURE AND SIMPLE

"...*Success—Pure & Simple* provides a blueprint for individuals to emulate towards success in what ever they endeavor to pursue. The book has helped me over a few tough spots."

—Tom Pollard, President
Human Resource Center, Ltd.

"...*I have found it very interesting and my wife who is sales oriented feels the same. It will hold a place of honor in my library.*"

—Steven A. Michalik
Mr. America, Mr. Universe

"...*It could be one of the books to live by!*"

—Edyie Tangreti
Editor, *Allegheny News*

"...*Your new book, **Success—Pure & Simple,** certainly represents an interesting concept.*"

—John Newman, Professor
Special Collections Librarian
Colorado State University

Success—Pure and Simple

Success—Pure and Simple

◆

How to Make it in *Business, Sports* and the *Arts!*

Dominic N Certo, KSJ

iUniverse, Inc.
New York Lincoln Shanghai

Success—Pure and Simple
How to Make it in *Business, Sports* and the *Arts!*

iUniverse books may be ordered through booksellers or by contacting:

iUniverse
2021 Pine Lake Road, Suite 100
Lincoln, NE 68512
www.iuniverse.com
1-800-Authors (1-800-288-4677)

Copyright © 1983 by Dominic Certo
Third Printing 1993 by Hillside Publications
Fourth Edition
Library of Congress number 83-90470

ISBN-13: 978-0-595-41671-4 (pbk)
ISBN-13: 978-0-595-67929-4 (cloth)
ISBN-13: 978-0-595-86015-9 (ebk)
ISBN-10: 0-595-41671-3 (pbk)
ISBN-10: 0-595-67929-3 (cloth)
ISBN-10: 0-595-86015-X (ebk)

Printed in the United States of America

To Those Spartan of Will
Warm of Heart
Singular in Soul
…And Especially to Martha & My Friends within this Book

Contents

What the Critics Say

At a time when it seems that the last thing the literary world needs is another self-help book, along comes Dominic Certo's *Success—Pure and Simple.* Therefore, the most surprising thing about this book is that it *is* needed, at least by those intrepid souls seeking to better themselves (aren't we all?) and excel in their chosen professions, and at life in general.

Certo, one of the last surviving members of that rare breed of self-made men, strives to explain to the reader how it is possible to overcome one's shortcomings by the power of self-control and inner desire. He relates his experiences in the areas of business, sports and the arts, the three disciplines he has excelled in. Through Certo's persuasive personal examples, and the tales he relates of others who have made it in their respective fields, the reader begins to garner an understanding of how it is possible to achieve that which seems unachievable.

Success—Pure and Simple will teach the reader how to use his strengths and weaknesses to the best advantage, regardless of his or her chosen field. Unlike the glut of self-help books on the market, this work seeks to motivate through actual examples, showing what can be accomplished once one puts one's mind to something. That is, after all, what a book of this genre should be, and this one is that, pure and simple!"

Russell Weiner
Managing Editor
Muscle Up, Muscle & Bodybuilder

Success—Pure and Simple explains to the reader the importance of determination and self-motivation. It's not just another one of those "How To" books authored by someone who has researched the best way to gain success and then conveyed those methods to you, the reader. But rather, *Success—Pure and Simple* is written by someone, namely *Dom Certo,* who brings the reader his own philosophies and guidelines straight from the heart. As a successful businessman, writer and athlete, Dom Certo gets down to basics. He tell you from his own experience and that of successful friends, what he has found to be the common denominator for success in business, sports and the arts. His bottom line theories won't be forgotten words skimmed off a page but instead are believable actions to fulfill your dreams. He doesn't tell you to do good or get better, he just gives you the insight and motivation, and from there it's Pure and Simple. *Success—Pure and Simple*—it could be one of those books to live by!"

Edyie Tangreti
Editor-in-Chief
Allegheny News

Foreword

Important Note Regarding This Edition of
Success—Pure and Simple

The accomplished individuals in this journal represent a collection of wonderful people, all of whom possess a genuine attitude toward growing their own success—and enjoying the trip. Some of those interviewed are the original participants, featured in the first printing of this book. These folks remain within because their advice and history still have relevance and merit. Some of the newly added individuals were selected to highlight some contemporary themes and to update the programs originally published in 1983, but all of those included are inspiring, active participants in the search for **success—pure and simple.**

Introduction

Is this book necessary? I'm really asking myself this question with honesty because if I don't believe it is, or if *I* have doubts, you, the reader, should have even more. Today, in 2006, I am especially careful in examining this question. With the idea of success having become so bloated and incorrectly defined, will my reissuing of a new edition of this book truly touch the hearts and minds of those in my intended audience? As I search for the answer, I see all the reasons why this book *is* necessary. For years my business career, sports and the arts have played important roles in my life. I have searched for excellence in each, for it is meaningless to participate to the fullest in things in which we have only a passive interest. I've met many men and women over the years who were great athletes, tremendous business people, and artists. Their accomplishments seem to form perfect composites of mind, body and soul. A great sampling of those individuals are in this book, as they have been generous and kind enough to share some of this wisdom and experience. Some have excelled as world leaders in one of the three areas, others in more than one, but all have notability in all three. Many are friends and some are acquaintances. All are wonderful people who have my deepest respect and appreciation. Many of the original interviews and thoughts of these special people appear in the pages of this book. Their words convey the strength of tried and true knowledge and wisdom. Although some of these thoughts show the variation in the times and, to some extent, technological development, the depth and value of what these great contributors believed in years past holds strong today.

As for me, I have been very fortunate to achieve relative success in each of the three areas of business, sports, and the arts. My background is illustrated throughout this book. But for now, let me make it clear that I did not come from a family of wealth, decathlon genes or aristocratic culture. My father was a construction worker, my mother, a domestic engineer who makes great spaghetti sauce and forever says, "I no gotta akcent." After serving with the Marines in Vietnam, I earned my college degree through the G.I. Bill, graduating in the top 10 percent of my class. I have competed in track, boxing, and bodybuilding on a national level, and have written three books, one that was nominated for the American Book Award. All of this happened while I maintained my business career and rose to executive management and national leadership. I was able to do this because my parents taught me independence, determination and self-respect (they also threw in love). But to that recipe, I added *desire. I WANTED TO BE SOMETHING! I WANTED MORE! I WOULDN'T SETTLE! I BELIEVED IN ME!* You can do it too, which is what this book is all about. Herein lie more than just my philosophies and guidelines. Also offered to you are the actual beliefs, personal tips, and practiced concepts of men and women who truly represent greatness in their fields. And finally, *Success—Pure and Simple* discusses those hidden questions buried deep down inside each of us that hold us back, keeping us from what we rightly deserve. It is my sincere hope that by the end of this book you will feel closer to yourself, knowing your weaknesses and strengths and therefore more inclined to develop the game plan of a winner!

We examine (together) three major areas of discussion: business, sports and the arts. This is a book of self-management and self-control, not so much in a technical sense but in its practical approach. I have tried to make *Success—Pure and Simple* a book for everyone. To answer my opening question: *Yes! This book is necessary!*

Maybe it's not so easy to be original today, but we can certainly perfect the originality and creativity that we *do* possess.

I wish you all, much success—pure and simple!

Dominic Certo, KSJ, 2006

1

Definition of Success

"No! Not another Self-Help book! Hasn't this all been said to death?" You're probably thinking that right now, but the fact that you have this book in your hands and are looking with curiosity at the material inside means you've got some interest, right? Let me start out by saying that there is nothing in this book that will *make* you successful. One thing and one thing alone delivers success: YOU! *Success—Pure and Simple* helps *you*. *Success—Pure and Simple* is a tool. It's a handy instrument that you will refer to whenever the need arises to be competitive, develop goals, manage your business or take charge of your life, formulate a results blueprint, or any other area that is covered on these pages. Success can be complex especially if we examine each facet of its diamond beauty. But we're not talking about the ends or results. We are talking about the means to its development. The road to success is simple and direct, once we formulate and adopt some of the attitudes mentioned herein, along with persistence and a healthy attitude toward the value of our lives.

Webster's Dictionary is quite simple in its definition of success: "a favorable or desired outcome of something attempted; a successful person, enterprise, etc.; attainment of wealth." Yet, this definition may not be in line with what we all perceive success to be. In many cases, wealth is not a goal but a product or result of the successful accomplishment. For example: becoming a successful actor or artist carries with it the appealing by-product of being paid handsomely for a job well done. In fact, in many cases, desire focused on simply achieving great wealth, absent the element of reaching for a specific goal, proves to be elusive, if not impossible. During the emotional movements of the '60s and '70s, our society developed a more relaxed approach to success. The prevailing attitude seemed to say "do your own thing" or "be yourself." Well, this concept is fine and can be used positively in making us comfortable while working toward our goals. But to strengthen that attitude, success seekers need a little more *meat* (or for vegetarians, *substance*). I would rather see the definition of success incorporate the obvious, with an added flair. For example: "Success—the interesting, challenging, and rewarding journey to a desired destination; making healthy goals and seeing them to completion; satisfaction, achievement or the effort put forth." I sincerely hope Mr. Webster might consider this logic more significant and make notes for the next updated version. How many times have we heard that "success is not the arrival but the trip along the way?" Haven't we all seen successful individuals breakdown and crumble or destroy themselves after they've "made it." Why? They seem to have everything they want. Their goals have been achieved. Shouldn't satisfaction and total bliss consume their lives? That seems reasonable. But it simply is not the case because the beauty, luster, excitement, and anticipation of success are in the actions and the plans we carry out. Yes, there are the moments of glory when we succeed. And it is impossible to measure the satisfaction, the emotional compassion behind those few moments when we finally revel in success. There is no pleasure or state of mind equal to that period of time when we first raise ourselves to a particular level of accomplishment. But the time and the feelings connected to it—that great emotional pay-off—is just not enough to sustain us through our entire lives. The joy we receive from any accomplishment can continue only if we go forward, setting new goals and making new efforts for greater successes. As human beings, we must prosper. We must develop. Otherwise, we stagnate. We must realize our worth as great living things.

Rather than defining success to great lengths, let's take a brief look at how some individuals see failure. One of the prime examples would be Thomas Edison with his remark, *"Show me a thoroughly satisfied man—and I will show you a failure."* Edison's comment points critically to the fact that once we discontinue having purpose, setting goals and new challenges, we lose the incentive to succeed. This idea supports my previous statement referring to success as the effort put forth, rather than the results attained.

Let's face it, there's no cigar for the loser, so by all means, my purpose or goal here is to help you become a *winner*. In keeping with Edison's idea, the amount of effort put forth will directly influence the effect. We must place greater emphasis on the actions we perform everyday in conjunction with our goals. A football team playing to win, using every bit of energy, strategy, and responsiveness they possess, probably will win, but if they don't, *was the goal any less worthwhile?* Were their actions wasteful, unproductive? Should they be embarrassed or dejected? *NO!* Not if they made every effort and response to the challenge. Not if they played well and showed the world that they were sturdy challengers. And not as they return to their locker room and feel that the better team won. They need only to enjoy the sweet passion of trying and nearly winning. And what about the next time? Might they be victorious because they are a better team for having competed in the previous game? Would they have felt as confident to challenge again had they not played as well? Success least appreciated is that which is the easiest to attain. Sometimes we have to sweat to our worth in order to improve. All too often, in our impatience, we expect immediate results. However, with immediate gains, we may become disillusioned with our goals. So, like a diamond that is set over and over again to enhance its beauty and value, we, too, must shine brighter with every new challenge.

One thing that is important to remember: There is no clear-cut path to success. There is no philosophy that binds us absolutely to rules regarding achievements. Yes, there are some guidelines or individuals that help motivate us. There are even premonitions, revelations, and inspirational concepts of success. But in spite of all of our best efforts, there will always be human mistakes. We all make mistakes, and if we accept our mistakes, past, present and future, and learn from these mistakes, we develop more than a thick skin; we marry wisdom. Always remember nothing is compulsory. Our goals should play the role of the healthy passion that makes our lives worthwhile, and if they do not, remember the words of W. C. Fields, *"If at first you don't succeed, try, try again. Then quit. There's no use in being a damn fool about it."*

2

Goals

Without a doubt, this has to be one of the most important sections of this book. Without goals, we are little more than a mere existence; we are all but lifeless, since the priority behind life is not so much to achieve, but to grow. Healthy growth can never be attained in the absence of goals. Many of us have goals without even realizing it, even though we don't consciously establish them, or write them down. Our nature and our drive are pointed in the direction of accomplishing something, whether to acquire a raise or promotion, marry our true love, put our children through college, or become wealthy and famous. No matter how great or small the goals, life is wasted without their direction.

Goals can be as basic as survival. In fact, for many people, at one time or another, survival has proven to be a very demanding goal. Rather than get into the "pyramid of goals" and how a basic law of survival evolves to more aesthetic and ego satisfying goals, I would like to utilize generalities and deal with the principles behind goals.

We all remember a particular time in our lives when were able to attain something that we desired. It could have been anything from a first job or a first date, to more demanding things such as, an athletic award or business award, and so on. Maybe it was just saving enough money to buy a bracelet for a special girl, or a set of tools for Dad. But at one time or another we set some goal in our mind that had to be achieved. Without a doubt, setting that goal brought excitement, pressure, anxiety or exuberance, but more importantly, it presented us with *purpose.* That purpose made life a little more worthwhile, if only to remind us of our feelings and wants.

I have noticed over the years that some individuals who suffer severe depression, mental strain, or boredom seem to have lost sight of making goals. A friend of mine, whom we will call Kirk, was once a great athlete and businessman. He rose from salesman to senior vice-president in one of the nation's largest companies. He had a wonderful family; a beautiful wife, two gorgeous daughters and an attractive and comfortable home in the suburbs. Kirk was always a happy individual, good-looking and witty. He had a charisma that radiated zest and excitement. But one day, Kirk met with a severe mental breakdown and was institutionalized.

What first comes to mind when I relate this story is the assumption that Kirk "was overworked." As a matter of fact, Kirk maintained his success with an eight-hour working day that was no more demanding than having healthy conversation, and dealing with some relevant paperwork. Kirk had achieved a degree of success through a system of goals that allowed him to work in an unpressured environment, but yet the man suffered a severe mental breakdown. He became institutionalized. This man, once a strong member of the community, of his company, and shoulder to his family, had somehow become a disabled and dependent shell. He has now has returned to work—as a street cleaner. A street cleaner? What happened? Well, at a meeting not too long ago, several salespeople were invited to a lecture on the characteristics of success. Kirk was also invited, by me, though certainly not as an insult to Kirk or the members of the audience. Kirk, in spite of his new profession as street cleaner, had begun to experience a renewed interest in life. He seemed more intense and energetic. He had become religious, and determined to enjoy his life. Kirk had an aura about him that resembled those earlier years when he met success around every corner. He even found enjoyment in his job as a street cleaner. He felt it had *purpose*.

As Kirk entered our conference room, he was well dressed, well groomed and smiling from ear-to-ear. No one in the room had any idea of his occupation, but they were informed of his previous achievements. Well, in short, Kirk did a fantastic job. He spent one hour lecturing on work habits and personal motivation, and showed a diagram of life that included goals. He opened his talk with a concept, that "from tiny acorns grow mighty oaks," and he placed emphasis on the personal satisfaction achieved in any endeavor, especially with family, work, and attaining good mental and physical health. Kirk received an incredible response and standing ovation by all the guests. In the weeks that followed, I was encouraged by everyone to have him return. I guess I've let you hanging. What happened?

Well, after that lecture, Kirk and I had lunch and while passing casual conversation, I paused, looked deeply at him and asked, "Kirk, what happened? Why? You had everything going. You were the last person I ever thought would cave in." Kirk didn't seem surprised or intimidated by my question. His broad smile softened a little and with a reflection of wisdom he looked down at his plate, back up at me and directly into my eyes, then said, "Nick, I stopped making goals."

And for that moment, I neither heard nor saw anything else; just the look of solidarity and conviction in what Kirk had said.

We both remained quiet for a few more moments. Then slicing into the silence as with a knife, he said, "Nick, I thought I had arrived. I thought I had become successful. I thought I was a success, and I lost interest in doing the things that made me successful. I was existing on my achievements, not wanting to do any more with my life. I had forgotten that success is not the destination, but the trip along the way." How true those words rang. Our luncheon lasted well into the middle of the afternoon. We talked at length about how important it was to set goals, no matter what the goals were. In his particular case, his goals had changed drastically from what they had been before he'd become disabled. Kirk suddenly nurtured an appreciation for the aesthetics of life, the fulfillment of a happy family, a dedication to God, even the satisfaction of cleaning streets. Yes, Kirk felt that even cleaning streets had purpose, and he did clean streets with enjoyment and pleasure. He explained how suddenly he had noticed people more, saw the outdoors and the changing of the seasons. Kirk felt that together, with the fruits of his work and the enjoyment of his surroundings, he was goal setting again—maybe not as lofty as they had been before, but Kirk was once again a fulfilled, happy, thriving individual who had purpose and happiness.

We all have a lot in common with Kirk. At one time or another, we all believe we have "arrived" or achieved what we consider to be our most important goals. But when this happens, we lose our "gusto" for life. We lose our *purpose,* as Kirk did, and we become somewhat empty and lifeless. This does not have to happen. We must develop an attitude in which we constantly set goals, so that when a goal is met, a new goal must automatically surface. In this way we never lose our appetite for life. These patterns, systems and attitudes toward goals can easily be achieved by following some simple methods. One method that I strongly feel contributes to understanding your life plan is to develop a system of setting *three* goals for every endeavor. They are:

1. Minimum or survival goal.

2. Real or attainable goal.

3. Dream or ecstasy goal.

And we must develop the habit of writing these goals down, because once written, the thought becomes a little bit more of a reality. The goals become clearer in our minds. The scriptive analysis becomes more embedded and the written record of the thought serves as a reminder and measuring rod.

Let's take a look at these three goal formulae:

1. *Minimum or survival goal.* The minimum or survival goal is just exactly that; the minimum goal that is acceptable for an individual's endeavor. For example:

> You are in sales. Your income is totally dependent upon how much you sell, in this particular instance, let's say insurance. Say for instance that you need a minimum income this year of $50,000 and your average commission per policy is $500. Simple analysis will show you that 2 times 500 will equal $1,000 per week, which means that you must produce two sales a week or approximately 100 sales per year (allowing for vacation). Since your income requirement is $50,000, this is your minimum need. For that reason, you must establish a *minimum goal* of 100 sales per year to survive.

Here's another example:

> You are a body builder or a weight lifter. You realize that to maintain your current physical development, weight, and general health, you must work out approximately three to four days per week for sessions of one to two hours. You also know that lifting within a desired weight range for a certain number of repetitions will allow you to maintain your current condition. With this in mind you set yourself a *minimum goal* of four workouts per week, with one to two hours in each session, using the necessary weight. This is your minimum goal for the year, the survival goal for that particular endeavor.

Here's another example:

> For the dieter. You have a minimum goal of losing 20 pounds in the next six months. This is the minimum you will accept. For that reason you divide the six months into *twenty pounds* and you come up with *3 1/3 pounds* per month, or approximately *3/4* of a pound per week. Breaking down the goal in this way makes the goal a lot simpler to see. Since weight loss is easier to achieve when planning it over a reasonable period of time, your minimum or survival goal becomes realistic and more easily attained.

Thus we see that minimum goals are boiled down to simple math. But we write them down for the purpose of recording what is clear in our minds and attested to on paper. It's best to avoid long explanations of your minimum goal. I list my minimum goal in large print, then, in one or two sentences, I break down its components. It is important to remember that a minimum goal is your rock bottom level of acceptance for any particular desire. We cannot go below our *minimum goals!* This is very important to keep in mind. Once we've registered this attitude, then the minimum goal is plugged into our thought processes. We move ahead with the actions that more than compensate for a *minimum survival effort.*

2. *Real or attainable goal.* Understanding that life has more purpose than just attaining a minimum or survival level, we feel the incentive to grow. For that reason, real or attainable goals are the most important of our three goals. Real or attainable goals allow for healthy growth from day to day, month to month, or year to year in any particular area that we have chosen. For example:

> Take the salesman who has to maintain a minimum goal of 100 sales per year to achieve an income of $50,000. What about inflation, the new car, possibly a vacation to Bermuda instead of the nearby shore? These are the kinds of things that make life a bit more comfortable, change the boredom and give some basic extra luxuries. While $50,000 is a minimum or survival goal, let's say $60,000 is what is truly desired as a means to protect against inflation and provide a little better vacation and family car for the salesman. Using the formula of achieving a minimum goal, based on 100 sales a year at a commission average of $500 per sale, we see that for a *real or attainable goal* of $60,000, we must divide 500 into $60,000. The new goal is 120 sales per year, which translates to a modest increase of an average of approximately 2 and a half sales per week, or around 5 sales every two weeks. The measure of success in this particular endeavor is based upon the small extra effort per week that will result in a more desirable goal.
>
> How about the body builder who is seeking to advance his physical level, and increase his lifting capacity enough to compete in his first contest, Mr. Western Solar System? He realizes while considering his diet, workouts, and amount of weight usage, that he must accelerate poundage and workouts by 10 to 15 percent. In this particular case, realism might dictate that he go from four to five workouts per week and gradually increase the weight so that he is successfully working out with 10 to 15 percent more weight. And so on down the line.

Real or attainable goals are goals that are more in line with what we should attain. Real or attainable goals require a small increase in effort over our minimum expectations in order to achieve what we truly want out of life. This degree of effort applies to any circumstance, whether it is dieting, for the overweight person, the runner trying to increase his average distance, or the manager who wants to take on a greater scope of projects each year. Each one has to break them down to easier, short-term formulas, so that results lead to success. How about the parents who are constantly trying to achieve communication with their children?

They can set a real or attainable goal of spending one more quality week each year with their son or daughter. This can be done by spending a little more than one half of a day more per month, or two hours on Sunday afternoon. Not much time to set as an objective, but the parent has added a whole week of quality time to that child's life.

In studying the *real or attainable goal* we not only have to generalize as to what we'd like to accomplish, we have to examine the quality of the improvement areas, and the efforts behind maintaining a continued *results-oriented action*. Otherwise, our little scientific endeavor becomes an exercise in futility. As with minimum goals, I generally mark in big letters what my real or attainable goal is. I underline with two lines to indicate the importance of that real or attainable goal, and I usually follow it with an exclamation point. The *minimum goal* generally has one line under it and no exclamation point. I write a few sentences, possibly one or two sentences more than for the minimum goal, giving a brief explanation of my real or attainable goal and how to break it down.

3. *Dream or ecstasy goal.* This probably needs the least explanation because as that smile comes to our faces this is the ultimate ideal; this is what we always dream about coming true. The salesman not making $50,000 or $60,000 this year but maybe $250,000 or $300,000, and the body builder who had dreams of becoming Mr. Western Solar System suddenly finds that his real or attainable goal is real and attainable. So for that reason he would love to entertain the objective of becoming Mr. Universe. The dieter who is pleased to attain that weight loss of 10 or 20 pounds and drop one or two sizes finds that establishing goals and working toward them achieves success, the result being a lean, toned person.

A mental exercise. Are these things we dream about? Well, yes and no. We certainly should dream about them—and we shouldn't consider them impossible. Why? Because that salesman who has prepared a plan for getting enough sales to achieve the real or attainable goal might come in contact with two or three very large business policies in which he will supply all of a product to an entire company, just due to the diligence and exposure of working harder and meeting more people. The two or three large policies might yield commissions equal to the total income of his *real* or *attainable goal.*

And the Mr. Western Solar System who increased his efforts by 10 to 15 percent to achieve his real or attainable goal has suddenly found a surge of power every workout that enables him to increase his efforts twofold, thus providing quicker and faster results, which put him in a position of holding greater capacity for higher level competition.

The dieter who set out to achieve a real or attainable goal by following a plan that allowed him or her to lose a certain number of pounds per week found a renewed surge of willpower that, together with exercise and a positive attitude, fostered even quicker weight loss.

The *dream* or *ecstasy goal* is possible, but only when our real or attainable goal is something we truly want to achieve. The *dream or ecstasy goal* combines the majority of the efforts we put together for our middle goals along with extra luck, timing and catalyst of spirit to achieve that result. The *dream* or *ecstasy goal* is very possible; if it weren't, there would be no great men and women throughout history. There would never be celebrities or leaders or contented and satisfied people. The dream or ecstasy goal is life's gift, after we're already satisfied. It's the extra enthusiasm that gives flavor to making goals and initiating efforts toward an improved life. *Dream* or *ecstasy goals* are "blue skies," or "pots of gold," that we dream about. Shouldn't that be a part of life too, even if it's the exception?

I follow the same procedure with the *dream or ecstasy goal* as I do with my other goals. I write it down in block letters or capitals. I underline it three times and put three exclamation points, and rather than add a few sentences I generally add one sentence explaining some of the catalysts that would make that possible. For example: DREAM GOAL; WRITE SUCCESS—PURE & SIMPLE!!! Make the extra effort to write every day for six months.

Thus, we have a general approach to the three main goals that should be targeted in each area that we are concerned with improving.

Next, I'd like to show you some additional methods of expanding on the goal process through the simple explanations of the individuals included in this journal.

Shakespeare imparts wisdom to us when writing, "Time is old justice, that examines all offenders." This is a simple fact with all great achievers. Some time back, the American Bankers Association clearly illustrated the problem picture of the average person's life. The facts they presented were disturbing but revealing. Of 100 individuals who started their lives at the same time, by age sixty-five, 38 would die, and 34 of those 38 would have left their families dependent on work, relatives, friends or charity. Only 4 of the 38 would leave their families financially independent. Carrying this analysis a little farther, 62 would be living at age sixty-five, and of those 62 *one would be wealthy—4 would be comfortable* and *57 would be dependent on work, relatives or charity.* Let's look at that again: *One* person out of a hundred will be wealthy, four will be comfortable and the four who have died will leave their families independent. *Ninety-one will have failed in their lives to achieve financial independence.* Sad and astonishing? Yes, it is disturbing, especially since we all believe that at some point in time we will make it; that our lives will change dramatically for the better. But facts prove that this does not always happen—rarely does it happen.

You ask why is one individual out of a hundred set to become wealthy and only four individuals more financially independent at retirement age? What did these individuals do that marked such a major difference in their lives? The answer is quite simple and basic. *Those that succeed, plan to succeed.* I repeat, they *plan.*

Let's try to illustrate this point more concretely. Picture your life as a house. You wouldn't begin building your house without a plan, would you? I mean you would need for blueprints to see where the rooms go, how the frame is constructed, where the windows fit and how you enter and leave and so forth and so on. Now if we tried to build your house without a blueprint we'd probably find ourselves immersed in confusion, chaos and poor structure. End result, the structure would be weak, if not totally collapsible. So why is it when we look at our life for all its beauty and value, do we allow ourselves to stroll blindly into the future with no plan or scheme? Why do we allow chance to be our life-long companion, instead of purpose? One of the greatest reasons this happens is because no one really cares whether we succeed or not. Yes, our family and friends would love to see us happy and successful. I am quite sure that our immediate family would encourage us to succeed and persevere, but no one else has a stake in the outcome of your life—no one *except you.* So, do we continue to languish in the careless attitude that robs us of success? Or, do we take some rudimentary actions that reflect the fruits of our existence, the fruits of our *success?*

One method, and we've all heard it before, is the Benjamin Franklin approach. That is, the listing of our assets and liabilities. What do we consider the strengths of our life? Are we strong financially? Maybe physically? Do we have intellectual or psychological strength? Assets come in many varieties. The same holds true for liabilities. The process of determining liabilities takes thought and honesty so sharpen your pencil. (By the way, not being a proponent of false humility or pride, I always encourage objectivity and honesty. Listing more than you got, or less strength than you truly have doesn't help anybody.) After listing your assets and liabilities, you have a choice. You can either keep this assessment to yourself or discuss it with a friend or relative. Having a frank discussion with a true friend or honest relative can help you truly determine whether or not the assets and liabilities you have assessed are truly there. After you have this clear picture, refer to it from time-to-time, day-to-day, week-to-week, remembering at all times to draw from your strengths in order to reduce your weaknesses. No matter what your goals are (and hopefully you have been specific), facing the reality of improving as a person will help you to succeed in your established goals.

The next step in providing a plan for your goal process is to *write your autobiography before the fact.* Outline what you envision happening within the next year, three years five years, and ten years, with a positive direction toward the goals you are trying to achieve. It is pointless to plan your life without a proper sequence of events tied into a period of time. If, for example, you realistically expect to finish college in the next two years and at that point attain your degree in say, economics, create the picture on paper of what your life will be like in two years: John Jones, a graduate of economics being interviewed for a position as a consultant to a financial company. In four years: John Jones taking additional courses in order to be considered for department head. In five years, John Jones, department head, controlling a division of twenty people, ten people, whatever the case might be. This method is the diagram, or the blueprint, we construct in order to make our house (life) exact to our plan. We can perfect this method even more by listing all our desires in a time sequence as fact, and checking along the way as time passes to see where our "roadmap to success" has taken us. We might even jot down how we would feel or anticipate our state of mind and our emotions at that achievement level, because testing the dream brings the reality closer and feeling success makes it more desirable.

Borrowing from Shakespeare again, he wrote the simple statement, "strong reasons make strong actions." If we don't have the reasons to be successful, there is little chance of "making it." As technology and automation increase at a faster and faster pace, originality decreases. Computers seem to advance us in spite of our limitations. For that reason, true success is a result of planning, rather than inventiveness. Imagination is always important, but imagination will never substitute for perseverance, diligence and design. *No matter how limited our talents, anyone can achieve success or prosper with earnest effort and controlled calculations.* We all remember the proverbial tortoise and the hare; all the talent in the world will never compensate for a concrete goal and relentless action.

In closing, goals must be planned and written down. They must be contemplated, developed and reset. Goals are instigated by our actions; they are our only weapon against time. There are no alternatives to goals. Remember the example provided by the American Bankers Association. Better yet, remember Thomas

Mann (for he says it better than I): *"Time has no divisions to mark its passing. There is never a thunderstorm to announce the beginning of a new month or year."* With that in mind, let's be prepared for the quiet visitor that comes and goes and leaves us no reprieve.

...to Review:

1. Set goals & write them down

    a. Minimum goal

    b. Realistic goal

    c. Dream goal

2. List assets and liabilities

    a. Be honest & thorough

    b. Assess the integrity of your list

3. Write your autobiography in advance for:

    a. 6 months

    b. 1 year

    c. 2 years

    d. 5 years

    e. 10 years

    f. at Retirement

Your Analysis Sheet
Secrets to Success

Assets	Liabilities

Goals (Career—Personal)

6 months
1 year
2 years
5 years
10 years
Retirement

Make Sure You Write It Down!

Part I
Business

Business and The Author

Some Business and News Features in Magazines about
the Author in earlier years.

MORTGAGE LEADS AWEIGH!

**Special Agent
Dom Certo recently
turned a mortgage
lead into a signed app
—on a 44' yacht**

Courtesy Impact magazine

Certo Makes Every Minute Count

Courtesy Allegheny News

In between lectures, competitions, contract meetings and
book tours, the schedule remains hectic.

Certo, far left, with Corporate Staff.

Certo outlines plans with his executive staff for new public programs.

Some Achievements

—Consistent "Million Dollar Producer"
Insurance sales. (Prudential Ins.)

—Winner of "President's Blue Ribbon Award" for sales three consecutive years. (ARA Services)

—Knighted twice into the Royal Order of St. John by Russia and The Netherlands

—Youngest Regional and National leader in management for four consecutive years. (New York Life)

—CEO and Principal of an International Service Management Company

—Lecturer, seminar conductor and consultant to several colleges, universities, professional athletes and large corporations

—Coach of the First International Bodybuilding Team to China and Hungary

—Listed in "Who's Who In The East & The World" 1981-1994

3

Business

Let's get down to it. Whether you're the struggling salesperson, over-burdened manager, or a juggling entrepreneur, we all seek to improve. Improvement can be measured by a promotion, increased business, or generally, more money. I don't think I would be remiss in assuming that the basic business mentality is motivated by (not greed—too tacky) financial remuneration, independence, and quite often, a wee bit of power or status. I don't get pangs of guilt or feel evil when I talk about money. Simply, it buys food, houses, boats, underwear, success books, toys for the kiddies, flowers for our sweethearts and an occasional get-away. It seems everyone uses it and the big challenge is to replace it as quickly as we use it up! Simple, yes, that's business. Everything is business today; sports, media, education, politics, even charities. The entire world, more or less, is driving toward capitalism. As people realize they have minds, imagination and the right to a certain quality of life, they become businessmen and women. My friend, you are not alone—everyone wants a slice of the pie.

A good businessman or woman realizes they contribute to the well-being of their families, the economy and themselves. They understand the blueprint of life and enjoy being a part of it. The one common ingredient in all truly successful business people is that they *make things happen!* They watch, observe and deliberate, but they also *act.* Once we realize that the true bottom line in business is *action,* we get the game plan. The next time you feel frustrated or stymied by your progress, analyze how much *action,* real action, you have taken. Sometimes there's too much smoke when we look at why one individual seems unsuccessful. In most cases, if that person funneled the energy into *acting* toward the goal instead of creating situations and 'smoke' that put the goal farther away, they would have all they desire.

No one wants to fail. Or do they? Psychologists have unmasked countless cases of people who sabotage their own progress for fear of success and its demands. But I believe that it has more to do with how we see ourselves. Most people feel they can create a picture of how they want people to see them, but they leave the real picture for themselves. In many cases, a person sees himself as less of a person than what they pretend to be. *Once we realize what we actually are, and become what we've been acting out for the benefit of everyone else, we start to take control of our lives!* We each have a hidden side, of course, and we each have a soul. I am not suggesting that the superficial day-to-day human facade should present our entire being. But for purposes of this book, and our quests to create successful profiles, consider this: The way we act *is* the way we are, or become! Frightening or exciting? Well, if you're frightened, thank God you bought this book! If you're excited, good for you! And either way, read on.

A few years back I had the good fortune of running one of the largest sales units in the country for a large national company. The people I selected were all different in personalities and profiles, but they all had one common ingredient—they seemed to love life and possessed the ability to believe in dreams. What is interesting though, is the fact that the more I write about the three sections of success—business, sports, and the arts—the more I see that one who strives has to be a bit of a dreamer. Endless, unproductive dreams are a waste of time. But golden rainbows that ignite adrenalin and produce action that develop results, turn out very lucky people. Some of those lucky people are in the pages that follow after their introduction. I have kept my own text brief in each section so as to complement the advice these wonderful people provide. I feel that countless chapters of "how to do this" and "how to do that" only turn into a Sunday lecture. I have been considerate enough to include only one or two vital areas to each subject, to keep matters simple (remember the title). It would take volumes and volumes of reference material to provide the technical background and insight to direct motivation in success in business, sports, and the arts. I would be presumptuous to even attempt it. But I do keep drilling the glaring points that all too often come up. One story comes to mind illustrating this point.

As a budding young salesman, I always kept an eye and ear open for the business giants, the top salespeople and managers who struggled to the top and made it gloriously. One particular individual was a speaker at a national sales meeting. I had followed his successful climb for some time and was amazed at not only his income and great sales batting average, but his genius in actions, planning and organization. Thinking in terms of the hundreds of ingredients and talents germane to his success, I approached him asking how he had done it…His answer was laughable but genuine: "*I get bored if I don't get better!*"

Harry N. Devlin

(Attorney-Instructor-Partner)
Westfield, NJ

Lt. Harry N. Devlin.

Harry N. Devlin today.

Harry is the senior partner in the law firm of Devlin, Norton & Derose, 114 Elm Street, Westfield, NJ 07090. The firm engages primarily in criminal, corporate and civil litigation. They handle many prestigious corporate accounts including Alpha Romeo and Fiat. They are one of the leading law firms in the country.

Mr. Devlin graduated from Syracuse College of Law with the Dean's award for Outstanding Student. He also received two jurisprudence awards for academic excellence. Harry was a Navy Lieutenant and served as a pilot in a Missile Control Center. His outside activities include teaching at Union College, flying as a private pilot, chairman of the Y. M.C.A. and the American Bar Association Cultural Law Committee. He is a member of New Jersey and New York Bar Associations.

The following statements impart his formula and beliefs:

The first element is motivation. Motivation is that intangible element which cannot be artificially induced. It must be there to attain success.

The second element is to establish attainable goals—goals that are meaningful to the individual. Goals that point to long-range and attainable ends. Winning within the judicial system is a result of preparation and not Perry Mason theories. That preparation must be effectively communicated in the courtroom, not only to the bench, but even more importantly, to the members of the jury.

Effective communication with the jury comprises the building blocks of communication. Convincing the jury to see the truth through good, honest, well-prepared and well-conveyed information goes hand-in-hand with attaining goals.

Communication is an ongoing challenge. Articulation—the learned ability to express one's self effectively before a jury is an essential element to good communication. This is not simple. It demands an understanding of whom you are dealing with. Juries are not made up of any socioeconomic conditions. Degrees of intelligence, varied backgrounds and personal prejudices are found in every panel. As an advocate, one may not adopt a condescending tone nor can one deal in esoteric terms. Dealing with the client is equally important and challenging.

A third element is flexibility. In law, flexibility must be regarded as an asset and as a key to a successful practice so long as it is handled from strength. Flexibility is a form of survival. When arguing a case and the facts are to your side—bang away on the facts! When law is on your side—bang away on the law, when neither is on your side—bang on the desk. Yet, the individual must constantly take stock to make certain that flexibility is not a disguise for a weakening approach.

A fourth element is awareness and to be alert to current trends in your profession. Have your trade publications sent to your home rather than to your office. A relaxed and uninterrupted atmosphere contributes to an easy recognition of problem-solving systems offered by these periodicals. Even a cursory scanning of such materials is immensely helpful in keeping abreast of trends. Be aware of your own strengths, talents and weaknesses. In the legal profession, there are situations which may require referral to a specialist. Don't be tempted to have your reputation diminished by attempting to handle a matter for which you are neither interested or equipped.

A fifth element: A choice of associates. Surround yourself with success! Choose people who have proven track records. Weigh the character of the people who will be partners or employees.

The difference between success and failure is having a totally qualified team.

Gerald C. Marrone

Lt. Col. And Corp. Exec., ret.
Redbank, NJ

Gerald C. Marrone retired as a senior executive from Quest Diagnostics, Incorporated in 2004. During his time with Quest Diagnostics, Mr. Marrone held the positions of Chief Information Officer and Chief Administrative Officer. During his tenure, Mr. Marrone was responsible for Information Technology, Real Estate, Purchasing, Human Resources, Aviation, the Corporate Program Office and Quest Diagnostics' Six Sigma program.

Prior to joining Quest Diagnostics, Mr. Marrone was a Division Executive with Citibank, N.A., from 1985 to 1997. Mr. Marrone served as Head of Global Data Center Services with responsibility for all Data Centers world wide in support of Global Finance. He also served as Head of Global Production Support, responsible for application development support world wide for Global Finance.

From 1980 to 1985, Mr. Marrone served as Vice President and CIO of Memorial Sloan Kettering Cancer Center in New York, and Vice President of Banker Trust Company from 1970 to 1980.

Mr. Marrone is also a retired Lieutenant Colonel in the United States Army.

Mr. Marrone holds a B.A. Degree in Political Science and Economics from the City College of New York, and an MBA from Fordham University. He is a graduate of the U.S. Army Command and General Staff College.

When asked what it takes to be successful, I have concluded over the years it is a combination of several things: luck, in the sense of being in the right place at the right time; having the right people working for you; having the knowledge to determine what has to be done and the fortitude to do the "right thing;" and lastly, the desire to excel at what ever it is you are doing.

I have observed over the years, that often really bright people fail to achieve what they are capable of because they are intellectually lazy and don't take the time to ask simple but direct questions about solutions. They assume the status quo as a given. Or, they look for complex solutions because they believe that it reflects on their ability if they produce a sophisticated solution. I have always tried to do the opposite. I try to determine the simplest solution to a given problem and avoid the complex whenever possible. I attempt to challenge the status quo to determine the underlying reason for a particular action or event. Often that can be determined by asking the easy question of why something is being done. I am frequently amazed by how often nobody asks that simple question and when it is asked the responses one gets. Answers like: because we always do it that way, or the policy is to do it that way, or the ever popular I don't know, are basically excuses for the status quo. Challenging these responses often leads to both simple and elegant solutions to long-standing issues which, when implemented, lead to organization effectiveness and efficiency. There is a risk in this approach. People are uncomfortable with change and, as a result, asking questions about the reason and way things work makes them uncomfortable. However, when you talk to really senior people in organizations, it has been my experience more often than not, they are as surprised and chagrined at the answers to those questions as I have been.

Organizations and people often have to be pushed to excel. Years ago I worked for William Aimetti, a senior executive at Citibank in the early 1990s. Bill always challenged those who worked for him to do more with less. One day, after a particularly difficult budget review and negotiation, I asked Bill how he could ask me to deliver what he wanted for the numbers he had put down originally. His answer helped me manage all types of organizations for many years. He said quite simply, I know you come to the meeting with numbers you are comfortable with. I also know that if I push you out of that comfort zone you will be creative and your team will be creative. In the end, you deliver more than you thought you could. My job is to challenge you. I have found that Bill was right; if you challenge good people you will be amazed at what they can achieve. The quid pro quo is you have to protect them and ensure that on the occasion when they fail that their efforts are recognized. Sometimes we can learn good things from failure. If you want people to take risks and be creative you have to allow them to fail, sometimes.

Years ago as a young Army Officer I had the good fortune to have as a senior officer removed me from a position that I thought I was handling as well, or better, than my predecessor. When told of the decision I was shocked. I didn't understand, as I had done everything the same way he had. I even had the same staff and supervisors in place to ensure continuity. Moreover, he had been decorated for the job he did. My boss told me that he had put me in the job because he wanted my thinking and approach. He didn't want me doing the job the same way it had been done before. Indeed he had been looking forward to the changes I would make to raise the position to a new level. I learned a few good lessons from that failure that have helped me my entire career. First, no matter who had the job before me I needed to take the time to assess the situation for myself and determine what and where changes were needed. Secondly, when you take a job, make sure you understand what is expected of you. Don't assume anything. Lastly, evaluate the people in the organization for yourself and remember you are only as good as the people who work for you.

The one thing I have always demanded of people who worked for me is that they do the right thing for the people and the organization. I expect every person in my organization to be treated with dignity and respect. In short, I expect my managers to treat others, as they would expect to be treated. I don't think there is any place for abusive managers in the work place and I believe that as a senior manager one of your most important tasks in this area is to lead by example and not tolerate the abuser no matter how well they do their job.

Gary Raymond

(Businessman-Inventor)
Rockaway, NJ

President Gerald Ford, Senator Courter & Gary Raymond

Graduate Riverside Military Academy, attended Lafayette College.
Former editor and author of Auto World.

Owner and president of Duostat Corporation, 114 Beach Street, Rockaway, NJ 08766. A multi-million dollar company specializing in graphic equipment and supplies. Duostat is an international leader in its field. A pioneer in his field, his product the Raymond cassette, would serve to revolutionize the industry and drastically enlarge their world sales.

Gary has been an entrepreneur since his youth selling newspapers, advertising and, yes, "used cars." he is truly a salesman, manager, and idea person. He takes pride in his company and friends. He also races stock cars and has won several events. Herewith his suggestions—

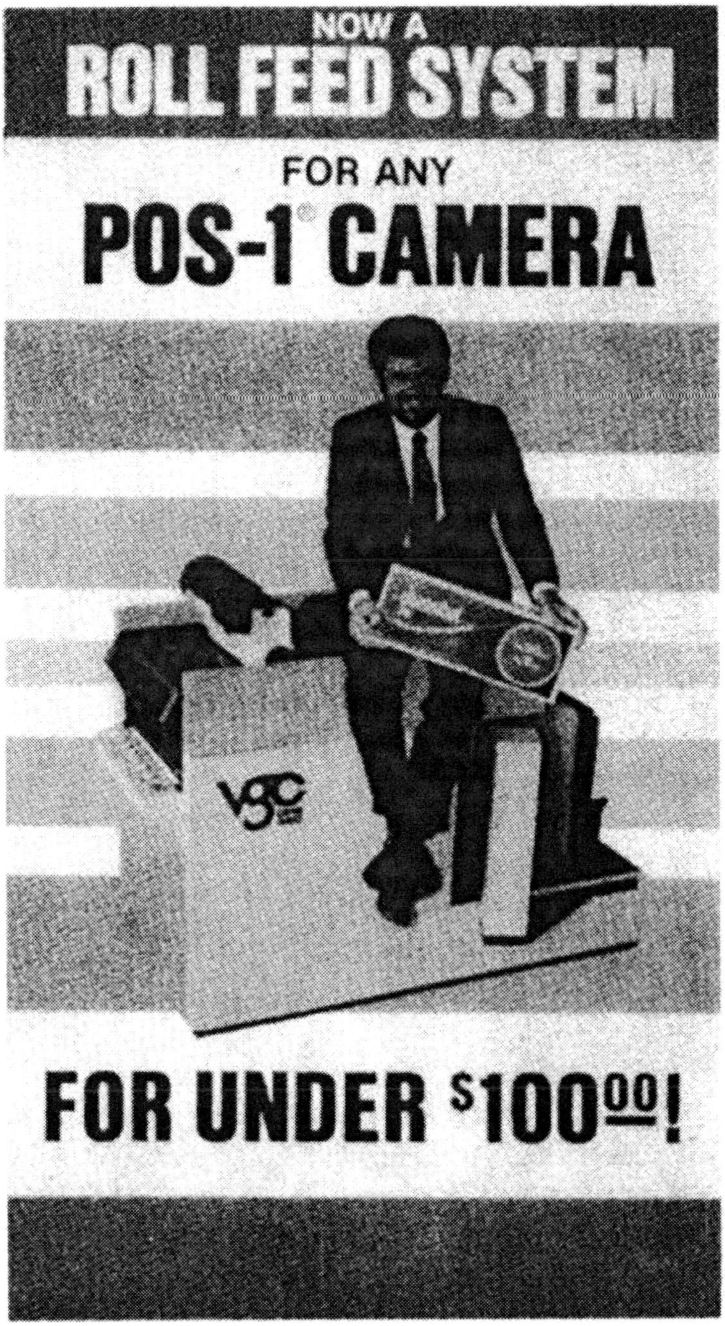
NOW A
ROLL FEED SYSTEM
FOR ANY
POS-1® CAMERA
FOR UNDER $100.00!

"I've always believed one should find something they're good at and run with it, whether it's writing, selling or kicking a football. My business has always been important to me. As a young salesman I always looked for a way to do something better. I never discounted the things I saw, I took them for value and looked for flaws, then ran with it.

Success at anything involves work. You have to get up early every day and hit it! You can only think about your ideas so long before you have to try them. First you start small, with what you have, then you parlay your winnings back into the pot to play for bigger stakes but you have to stay with your winning formula.

Never ignore people, we need them desperately. I am very loyal to my employees and friends, there is something to be said of genuine loyalty and consideration for other human beings. They understand it, can tell if it's sincere or not and respond accordingly. I have been fortunate enough to have friends and associates who believe in me and my concern for them. Always reward hard work and loyalty and it will remain with you.

Getting back to ideas. Go with a good one, believe in it, see it through, keep improving it—but don't reinvent the wheel!—Always keep your business pocket separate from your personal pocket and if one is empty try not to take from the other.

Remember hard work, be loyal to friends and associates, parlay your winnings, and do what you're best at. Find a good idea and make it better or in simpler terms *If It Ain't Broke, Don't Fix It!*"

Jay J. Freireich

Partner, Poe and Freireich, Law Firm, Celebrated Tax Attorney.
Florham Park, NJ

Jay J. Freireich, was born in Atlantic City, New Jersey. He graduated from York University—Canada with a B.A., obtained his Jurist Doctorate from Nova University School of Law and received his Master of Laws in Taxation from the University of Miami. He is a member of the Bar in Florida, Pennsylvania, and New Jersey. He is also admitted to practice before the United States Supreme Court, the United States Tax Court, the U.S. Court of Federal Claims as well as many United States District and Circuit Courts.

Mr. Freireich has argued cases successfully before the United States Court of Appeals and has even filed a tax case in the United States Supreme Court. He helped Congress rewrite the innocent spouse provisions of the Internal Revenue Code. He has aided many clients to successfully resolve or win outright multi-million dollar tax issues.

Many cases that Mr. Freireich has handled have appeared in publications includ-ing the New York Times, New York Post, Newark Star Ledger, New Jersey Law Journal *and* National Law Journal. *Jay J. Freireich has appeared on ABC's, Good Morning America as a tax expert in a segment involving the new innocent spouse tax law. He also appeared as a general tax expert on CNN in a feature story on general income taxation.*

Another personal highlight for Mr. Freireich was taking the two-day deposition of Don King in a case involving a business dispute over boxing promotional rights.

Mr. Freireich is married with two high school-age daughters. He is an avid tennis and table tennis player. He is active in his Temple and was a former co-president of its Brotherhood.

Mr. Freireich is a partner in the firm of POE & FREIREICH, P.A., a tax and business law firm that handles virtually any tax or business related matter. The firm consists of seven attorneys and has offices in Florham Park, New Jersey; Mineola, New York; and Scottsdale, Arizona. As a boutique firm, concentrating in the areas of tax and business, the Poe & Freireich is able to provide its clients the hands-on, personal service they expect from a small firm, yet the specialization and sophistication they would expect only from a larger firm.

Before commencing the journey to success, you must first evaluate your own strengths and weaknesses. Early on in my career, I understood that my strengths are my reasoning and problem solving ability and my practical straightforward approach. My weakness is my bedside manner. If someone presents me with a bad case, I tell them. I have never been good at telling my clients just what they want to hear.

The key to success certainly involves exploiting your own strengths, while, at the same time, actually turning your weaknesses into strengths, too. Certainly a business and tax lawyer must have natural reasoning abilities. Problem solving must also be a key ingredient in your makeup to excel in this field. Without exceptional reasoning and problem solving skills, you must look to a different field to find your successful niche.

Next, you must learn how to use your weakness to an advantage. I have been able to turn my greatest weakness into a strength. I have learned that many, if not most, clients actually want to hear the truth. The ones that want to hear only what they want to hear do not stay with me as clients very long, for they do not get the service they want.

However, I have been able to build my practice with the majority of clients who want to hear it straight. They do not want to hear me sugar coating how the problem in their case is not real.

I believe I have become successful by giving my clients consistent, pragmatic and accurate advice. My bedside manner is still rough around the edges, but my clients seem to prefer that approach.

To be successful, we must not concentrate solely on books and research but, rather, focus on the human aspect of dealing with people. Knowledge of the subject matter through hard work and study are a given. But to really take your success to another level, you must put yourself in the shoes of those people whom you represent. You must feel what they are feeling and imagine what they are going through. You must understand their business. It is by doing all of this, that you can better serve your client and thereby succeed.

Gloria Bloomfield

(Financial Consultant—Sales Executive)
Fords, NJ

President and owner—Bloomfield Associates.
Financial Counseling, Estate Planning and Insurance Brokering.
Woman of the Year, 1973-Fords Womens Club
Agent of the Year, 1977 and 1979-New York Life Insurance Co.
Member of the prestigious *President's Club-New* York Life Ins.
President of the *Edison Chamber of Commerce*

"In 1973 I started my sales career as the first woman broker in an office of over 40 men. *Dom Certo* was my Sales Manager and personally hired me. At the time it seemed rather ominous since I was trailblazing and facing several obstacles but he believed in me as I did in myself and that helped give me the extra edge. Raising 3 children on my own was no easy task and the necessity to succeed was ever present but I set goals right from the start and worked out plans to achieve them. I tackled my weakest areas of self-discipline and organization by admitting to myself they were a problem. Once I realized that I needed work, the job at hand became simpler. I always raised my self-confidence with each success and within 3 years I began to lead the entire office in an agency that was the biggest in the country.

A few points I feel are worth sharing: I made a commitment to myself and my goals. I never thought of quitting...*Never!* When things got tough I just *worked harder.* Always believe you are unique and special—that self-belief helps to motivate you to an upward climb. Elevate your attitude, your work habits, your goals and the company you keep. Look for the best in people and remember the old saying "As you associate, so you become."

John A. Lepore

GIOVANNI
Chief Operating Officer
The Certo Group, LLC and L.A. Cafés
www.thecertogroup.com
Westfield, NJ

John Lepore serves as Executive Vice President and Chief Operating Officer of The Certo Group, LLC and L.A. Cafés.

John heads the L.A. operating team as it endeavors to grow in all areas of the company. John's varied background brings great talent to both L.A Café's and The Certo Group.

Mr. Lepore, a former law student and graduate of The University of Rhode Island, began his career with the Judiciary Department of Rhode Island. Early in his career, he discovered that he preferred making people happy with food rather than subpoenas, thus the move to our camp.

John served as President and CEO of both large- and medium-sized companies, including his own Sierra Foods. Many of you might remember John as President and CEO of Foods Concepts and Automatic Catering, where he brought a $5 Million dollar company to over $100 million in sales by 1988. John also spent many years as the Vice President and General Manager of Holiday Inns, where he rose from a Chef Manager to Executive Director for their numerous hotel-restaurants throughout the company. He obtained many industry, commercial and community awards. He also has been a feature speaker at Johnson and Wales University and other fine Culinary Institutions. John has managed as many as 2000 employees and as little as 80, so his abilities are exceptional for any task and structure.

John's son is a District Manager for Compass Group and developed many of his skills while working and training in John's companies.

Mr. & Mrs. Lepore reside in lovely Westfield, NJ.

My career started when I was fourteen years of age working in my dad's summer restaurant in Narragansett, Rhode Island. I realized that to persevere in this industry you must have a solid work ethic.

After I finished school, the Superior Court of RI employed me where multi-tasking became very important. I had to work in the courtrooms, offices, and the lockup. It was never boring.

In 1968 I went to work for Holiday Inns. They were the #1 hotel chain in America. I was very fortunate that I had a mentor who taught me the hotel business from the bottom on up. I set my goals for my new career. I worked long and hard. I listened carefully and kept my thoughts to myself and learned. In 1980 thru 1982, I was the General Manager for a top-ten hotel in the Holiday Inn system.

In 1983, I moved from Florida to New Jersey to work for Automatic Catering. Even though "change" is the most feared word in the English language, I happen to adapt well to change. This move meant that my family, who means the world to me, had to move. We have always had a strong family with consistent deep faith. In 1985, I was made President of Food Concepts, which eventually became a 125 million-dollar food service company. I have stayed in the food service area for over twenty years. I have learned that nothing replaces loyalty and a respect for other people.

Wayne S. DeMilia

(Movie Producer-Sports Promoter-Entrepreneur)
Long Island, NY

Craig Perry and Wayne DeMilia producers of Pumping Iron II.

Wayne DeMilia is the associate producer of the film Pumping Iron II. He is the world's leading sport promoter in pro-bodybuilding for women and men—coordinating several events a year: including the World Cup, Grand Prix and American Championships seen regularly on ABC Wide World of Sports and NBC Sportsworld. Wayne has been seen and interviewed on several major networks and top shows including P.M. Magazine. He owns and manages several companies including Physique Productions one of the most successful bodybuilding promoter-management companies in the world. In 1984 he brought bodybuilding to the Radio City Music Hall for the most prestigious title event worldwide, "Mr. Olympia." He started his pro-bodybuilding circuit in 1978 and has grown dramatically ever since. Wayne is a graduate of Queens College City University with an A.S. in engineering, a B.A. in communications and a B.A. in political science. Everyone who is familiar with DeMilia speaks highly of his dedication, honesty and integrity in a sport and business that is competitive and demanding. Herewith his advice and background for any entrepreneur:

"I've made it to this stage because I will not accept defeat. If I lose it is because I just ran out of time. I only get involved to win, otherwise it's not worth the effort and heartache. You can get anything you want if you plan it and believe in the plan. See yourself succeeding, forget about failure, if you plan to fail...you will.

Always remember as a businessman, promoter or manager, to expand your contacts. Learn to associate with successful people. Feel comfortable with them and let the atmosphere become habit. Then be loyal to those friends and individuals whom you respect. Remember your roots and your integrity. Expect the same from those you befriend.

Try to be a good judge of people. Don't be suckered into a relationship with people who will drag you down, waste your time, or 'slur' your name. You can very easily fall into that rut and find yourself going backwards. Try to develop a radar for people that are worth your time, respect, and consideration.

Always broaden your horizons, reset better goals and increase your abilities and capacity to learn and accomplish more. The higher up you go the more there is to accomplish and the tougher the competition. Keep your company economically sound and cost conscious. Manage it well and it will pay you back.

Finally work hard. That's *Pure and Simple* in itself. Combine working hard with working *smart* and you've got the formula. Nothing will be accomplished through weak or half-hearted efforts. Get up every day and tackle the task at hand. You solely put the wheels in motion.

Remember, Dreams Can Come True! *Certo* and I laughed about events that developed in the years since our first competition together, and how we planned to see bodybuilding emerge as big "box office" with worldwide acclaim. All too often great dreams that seem preposterous in the fetal stages have a way of surprising us.

I like to celebrate after a great accomplishment or victory. I usually find myself with my friends, laughing and toasting the moment. *After all, isn't that a good part of what it's all about? Good Luck!*

Wayne DeMilia with Miss Olympia Rachael McLish

Peter C. DeRosa

CEO, Jost Financial Intl.
Greenbrook, NJ

Mr. DeRosa was educated at Western Kentucky University, earning a BA in Economics and Psychology, and then went on to earn his Masters at Rutgers in Economics and Finance. He started his career as a financial planner within a large insurance company, Home Life Insurance which merged with Phoenix Life Insurance Company in 1991, where he quickly rose to perform within the top 1% in the world. Peter began doing comprehensive financial planning for high net worth individuals and public corporations in 1980 and became a Certified Financial Planner specializing in estate planning and investment management. By 1984, he had formed Jost Financial Management Corporation, an investment advisory firm that manages money for individuals and corporations both public and private.

In 1982, Peter DeRosa was inducted in the Home Life Hall of Fame, carrying with it membership in the prestigious group of both high level producers and those exhibiting a proven desire to help others in all walks of life. A true demonstration of humanity and a giving of oneself for the benefit of others is an essential prerequisite to being invited into this elite group of individuals.

Mr. DeRosa has been invited to give seminars at Fortune 100 companies on financial topics and what one can do to truly achieve success in life.

This is what Pete has to say about success:

Success in my opinion has always been a state of mind. It is not only about wealth accumulation it is about being honest with one's self and know what truly is important in life. What will it take to make me happy? I have always felt that even in my business in dealing with clients in all walks of life and in different parts of the world it comes down to feeling good about how you lead your life and doing the right thing. I learned early in my advisory practice to never give advice that I would not follow in the same situation. It's not just about making a sale or getting a client. I have always felt money comes much easier to those who combine hard work with a sense of well being. If you don't like yourself or what you have become in the process of accumulating your wealth, you will never achieve true success.

Of course, financial well being can lead to the security that is important to most of us. To provide for our families and give them what they need to get ahead in life. To me this has been the strongest motivating force toward hard work and dedicating myself. I always felt the desire to leave something behind for those I love. This deep-seated belief has always motivated me to help others achieve the same important objective. In short, believe in what you do. **Take the time to constantly learn about new developments in your profession or career and share these ideas with others who can use them.** Knowledge within your profession is extremely important, but being able to convey a sense of sincerity with your clients, customers or others you come into contact in business is the strongest element leading to success. There are many intelligent, even brilliant people who never achieved the success they might have. In dealing with people, I have always found they don't only care about what you know. What they really want to know is how much you care. In my experience in dealing with people, this basic tenet holds true.

Success is about achieving personal satisfaction with one's life. It's enhanced when one has a balance in life. Work should not be our only source of satisfaction. Take the time to enjoy yourself whether it be travel or other new experiences that can bring excitement. In short have some fun and keep a good perspective on what you are working for. Try to enjoy what this life has to offer while you are still healthy enough. Our minds need refreshment and exposure to new surroundings and experiences. Success in its purist form is not only measured by accomplishments but also the contentment we derive from how we lead our lives and how well we enjoy it.

Charles B. Crane

(Corporate Executive)
Philadelphia, Pennsylvania

Graduate Rutgers University, 1966.
Foresight Scholarship winner in college for sales ability. Sales Vice-President of major international service company at age 33. As a vice-president of sales he reduced sales expenses by over 30% and increased sales by 40% for two consecutive years.

"Chuck" substantially improved success patterns of mediocre salesmen into top producers. He was recipient of Governors Leadership Award presented by former and late Governor Ella Grasso. Currently Chuck heads marketing and research as regional manager for the Macke Co. of Philadelphia. Herewith his suggestions—"I have always felt that the key to selling anyone anything, whether it be a tangible product or an intangible service, is to make that product or service solve a particular problem. It does not matter if the problem is real or perceived as real. The sales person who gets the order, gets it because he has found the solution with his company's product or service.

In many situations the customer's problems are not always apparent. Sometimes the customer may even have a troublesome situation of which he is not aware. A truly professional sales representative becomes knowledgeable to the potential sale by asking questions and by keen observation of the situation. In effect the sales representative becomes a consultant to the prospect because he can provide the correct solution.

The pitfall of many potential super sales reps is that they never drop the role of consultant and totally forget that their objective is to sell. The consultant will recommend effective solutions through a variety of sources, whereas the salesmen *must* find a solution with his company's product. In effect, many salesmen perform a free consulting job for the customer at their own company's expense, and are amazed when the prospect buys his solution but not his product.

The service that my company provides is professional management of large at-work cafeterias. In many cases, we look at major investments in redesign and equipment purchases. I will never forget the work I put in trying to sell a major state university, a job that would have meant a very large commission check. I provided drawings, cost sheets and solutions to numerous problems. I did everything but sell my company and the benefits it offered. The potential sale vanished and I thought I had done everything right.

How many times have you worked your tail off only to lose an account to another salesman who you thought spent little time selling the company? Consider the fact that he was *selling* and you were consulting, not stressing the benefits of doing business with your company."

Remember—solve the problem with the benefits that only your company can provide and you will make the sale! *"Success—pure and simple."*

Robert Lee Putnam, Jr.

(Businessman—Master Carpenter—Licensed General Contractor
—Real Estate Investor)
www.michaelrobertsconstruction.com

Robert is co-owner of Michael Roberts Construction, Inc., as a General Contractor in Northern California's Bay Area. Putnam began his professional journey with the completion of an apprenticeship program with the Carpenter's Union Local 152. He became the youngest person to complete the four-year program by finishing at the age of 20. Robert then climbed the ranks at one of the largest Union framing construction companies in the Bay Area, Jonce Thomas Construction. He went on to become a Superintendent with a high-density multifamily construction company, Bay Area Apartments Communities, where he learned to train and mentor subordinates to benefit the employees as well as the company. During this time, Robert opted to broaden his horizons and attended and graduated from the National University for Construction Management. With 21 years in the construction business, Robert co-founded Michael Roberts Construction, Inc., and began to investigate and diversify into real estate development.*

In his own words, here is Robert's story:

I was born in June of 1967, the fourth of five siblings: four boys and one girl. My father was a self-employed builder/developer and an electrical contractor by trade. Growing up in the '70s and '80s, I experienced life in the upper economic class. Due to the rising and falling of the economy in real estate, I also personally experienced middle class life and the pressures of extreme poverty. Near bankruptcy eventually struck when my father was unable sell his development of homes in the early 1980s. The interest rates inflated to 21-22% and left most of the population unable to afford a home. I was the oldest son still living at home. The effect on a 14-year-old boy was devastating at first:

- The bank repossessed all of the homes.

- As a result, the family moved multiple times to and within various states to survive the recession and support the family.

- I traveled with my father and worked on whatever projects he could find just to make a living.

This turn of events made for an excellent learning and life experience, helping me become a more independent and responsible child. With no opportunity for college, I obtained a G.E.D at the age of 16 and began an apprenticeship with the Carpenter's Union.

With all the adversity and financial hardship, my father still, to this day, proclaims that real estate investment is the best way to earn a living. After all, he was extremely successful in the '50s and late '60s in this area. "You have to have money to lose money. More money risked for larger gain may result in greater loss." I determined to trust his words of wisdom; however, I would be more cautious and make my financial moves with better risk management. I was able to learn much in the construction field while climbing the management ladder at one of the largest framing companies in California. By the age of 23, I had run many large projects in the role of superintendent.

Loyalty is one of my most valued qualities; I worked with Jonce Thomas Construction from the age of 17 to 31. Mr. Thomas taught me how to be a leader and how to build a myriad of projects. I built schools, churches, hospitals, apartments, condominiums, and many other types of structures. With a desire to expand my horizons, yet not ready to branch out independently, I took a position with a Real Estate Investment Trust Company (Bay Apartment Communities) as a Project Superintendent. The company built vast, high-density, multifamily construction projects ranging from $30-120 million, including as many as 500 to 750 dwellings. Still the youngest person in my field, I was able to develop newer means and methods for production, contractual documentation, scheduling, and many other pertinent aspects of the business while operating within a very old system. I decided to continue learning, in order to go beyond hands-on training. I attended three years at the National University for Construction Management and graduated in 1999 while at the same time, investing in rental properties. This effort continues today, and I am presently an officer of two Homeowners Associations.

The high-volume, high-paced, large-scale construction experience coupled with my construction schooling helped me make the decision to take my career to the next level. At the age of 33, I passed the California State Board of Contractor's test and took the first steps toward developing my own business. In 2001, I partnered with a long-time co-worker, Michael Avila, to form Michael Roberts Construction Company Inc. Memories of my teen years, struggling side by side with my dad just to make ends meet, were foremost in my mind. To continue to entrust my future in a business that broke my father's back, his will, and the bank, I was driven to move our firm through the partnership phase and into a Corporation to protect our personal assets. This was a huge step for a tradesman with limited academics but, I have always felt that there is more than one type of education!

MRC, Inc. progressed from $350,000 gross in 2001 (the first year in development) to $80,000,000 gross in 2006. For the short time we've been in business, a few of the most valuable lessons learned to run a successful construction company, I believe, are:

1. Be the very best at what you do.

2. Have a strong work ethic. No matter how intelligent or aggressive one may be, without a good work ethic, you will not succeed. Your employees are watching and will emulate what you do and how you conduct yourself.

3. Teach your employees everything they need to know to make them and the firm successful. Never be afraid that they will look too good or take your job. Set realistic mutual goals and stick to them. Finally:

4.   Invest and think long term. Invest in real estate and invest as much as can be afforded in your 401K and/or retirement plan.

My career is and always will be important to me; however, it's not the most important thing in my life. Happiness is the definition of success. Creating a balance of all things that bring me joy will surely be my greatest achievement. Confucius once said: "Choose a job you love and you'll never have to work a day in your life." This simple statement is the basis for continuing in the construction industry in spite of the risks. For me, a well rounded, balanced life not only includes business but family, friends, health, hobbies (which include bodybuilding, snowboarding, wakeboarding, motocrossing and riding my Harley) and community.

My greatest accomplishment, without sounding cliché, is definitely my family. Nothing compares to the unconditional love that I receive from my beautiful wife, Laurann, and my 18-month-old son, Chase. With each aspect of my life fulfilled, I'm happy and I'm successful, pure and simple.

Robert Kennedy

(Publisher-Author)
Brampton, Ont. Canada

Publisher of one of the top selling physical culture (exercise, nutrition, bodybuild-ing) magazines in the world.

Like many entrepreneurs, he started from nothing and built his business step by step. He is also author of some two dozen books, including his best sellers "Hardcore Bodybuilding "and "Beef It!" (Sterling Publishers, NYC) Bob is credited with invent-

ing the acclaimed "Pre-Exhaust System," a bodybuilding technique which develops a Mr. Universe type physique. Says Kennedy...

"If there is any advice I would consider to be important to the aspiring entrepreneur I would suggest that he or she make themselves as familiar as humanly possible with the area or subject in which they wish to excel. You cannot know too much, and the only way to find out is to read everything you can lay your hands on...study and take courses if possible and ask questions from those who know more than you do. Make yourself *the* expert and then you will have established a base from which to work...upwards to success.

Another factor which I consider relevant is to resist trying to become a success using an untried formula. True, a few geniuses have breezed through to the top of the ladder using unconventional methods, but they are definitely in the minority. Why try unproven ground when a pathway has been laid by others? Artists, publishers, sportsmen, businessmen...can all study the form and methods used by others to get to the top. Imitate or copy these people. As time goes by your individuality will come through and as you climb the ladder of success, perhaps these same people will in turn be influenced by *your* methods. A success formula is a success formula...is a success formula. Do *not* change that which already works.

Finally, as a publisher of a bodybuilding periodical *Muscle Mag International*, I came into contact and became a firm friend of oil Billionaire J. Paul Getty, himself an ardent enthusiast of bodybuilding, weight training and strength performance. Getty didn't much like being labeled the world's richest man (which he was!) but really preferred to be known as an entrepreneur. He was excessively shy about his looks and didn't appreciate the publicity his wealth afforded, especially when he was labeled a recluse, and worse than that, a *mean* recluse. Neither description was true. Up until his death in 1976 he was constantly surrounded by friends, family and business associates, and his generosity to those he liked was well known by insiders.

He did, however, resent being *used* by people (especially if he did not even know them) and hence when he gave over his country home (Sutton Place, Guildford, England) almost each weekend, to charity groups so that they may hold fund raising parties, he was duly upset by the fact that literally thousands of dollars was being charged to his phone bill, by so-called fund raising do-gooders who took advantage of phoning all over the world, no doubt to boast that they were in J. Paul Getty's home and that he was paying the bill. When Mr. Getty finally tracked down some of these phone calls he even found that many were in fact transatlantic *business* calls…all no doubt charged with a prideful smirk to J. P. Getty himself.

His action was legendary. Getty installed a pay telephone in the section of Sutton Place that was loaned out to charities. The world press had a field day. He never lived it down, even though he supplied a bowl full of change so that the charity organizers could make local calls free of cost. (This was never reported in the press.)

It should be added too, that any house guest of J. Paul Getty's was welcome to use any one of a dozen other phones, to call anywhere for as long as they wanted.

But business was business in the Getty offices. In spite of being the richest individual on Earth and being involved in one of the higher profit making ventures of all…Oil, J. Paul Getty had a saying which he lived by. "No business can build or survive without a strong sense of thrift."

William F. Loehning

(General Manager—New York Life)
Barrington, Rhode Island

Graduate of Newark State College with a B.A. Degree in Social Science, was Pres-ident of the Student Body and was listed in Who's Who Among American College Students. *He entered the life insurance business in 1970. Today he is a General Manager for New York Life Insurance Company. His agency is responsible for all marketing activities in the state of Rhode Island, Southeastern Massachusetts and*

Northern Connecticut. He has won the General Agents and Managers Associates National Management Award for the past three consecutive years and has also received numerous company awards and citations for agency growth and management. He is the Secretary/Treasurer of the General Agents and Managers Assoc. of Rhode Island, a member of the National Association of Life Underwriters and the Rhode Island Society of CLU's. Mr. Loehning earned his Chartered Life Underwriter designation from the American College in 1982 and is currently enrolled in the Certified Financial Consultation program. He also is a member of the Board of Directors of Summer Industries, Inc. an upcoming company that features quality baby products.

"It is my belief that success in life many times comes from one's response to the negative events in someone's life as opposed to the positive ones.

In business those people that I have deemed most successful were the ones who could recover the quickest from a setback, gain strength from it and turn it into a positive situation.

In my own life my father's untimely death when I was 16, which at the time was a devastating blow to me, has become the most positive driving force behind my limited success.

When a person is forced into a negative situation beyond his or her control, it is amazing the amount of inner strength that one can muster when called upon to do so. Unfortunately in many instances, people do not reach for this inner strength. It is there in all of us, one just has to be willing to reach for it.

The difference between being average and above average in life is a mental decision. Most people are happy being Indians and not chiefs—others say they want to be chief but are not willing to pay the price."

4

Showpersonship and Selling Ideas

Salespersonship rather than the archaic and traditional "salesmanship" is more the mode de temp since so many of our successful people today are women. I've had the good fortune in my career to work with and manage a few exceptional women who displayed extraordinary talents in an area of sales that, for years, was dominated by males. Women play an important part to this challenging game we call sales and their place in the marketing game is challenging and complex. For the time being, let's take a look at a characteristic of salespersonship that is important to business.

First of all, the old adage, "A good salesperson is a born salesperson" is too convenient. Today's buyer, be that person an individual buying personally or for a business, is more in tune to a logical series of circumstances and solutions that bring that person to a decision. This is contrary to the once emotional "hard sell." (I would like to add, though, that logical solutions and modern strategy do not always facilitate a sale. There is still that degree of clever, strategic and honest showpersonship that gives weight to making the sale.)

The salesperson of today is a professional in every sense of the word. He or she is faced with a long list of demanding characteristics that they must possess in order to be successful in their chosen field. This list includes their involvement with management, professional accountability, problem solving, general administration, marketing research, oral communication, written communication skills, inter-company development, and industrial development, with the list going on and on. It is quite obvious that the salesperson of today is not the peddler of yesterday. Just as the lawyer, doctor, engineer and accountant are not born, neither is the salesperson. He or she is not a product of their natural inheritance. For these reasons, I've outlined different areas that the salesperson should put forth in their diagram to develop a professional sales career.

59

For now, my major concern in this particular section of my book, is the area of showpersonship. The salesperson or businessperson who puts forth the extra effort in closing a particular sale will be the person who receives the sale. And what are the extra efforts that a salesperson can put forth? Well, the standards of being punctual, looking neat and clean, communicating adequately with the jargon of the market, doing the preliminary research, rehearsing, knowing possible objections to the sale on the part of the prospect and how to overcome them, presenting responsive solutions that satisfy the prospect's needs and moving toward a firm and expected close. I say *"expected close"* for a very serious reason. If the professional salesperson does his or her job adequately, puts in the required time, does the necessary research and soothes a prospect's objections with viable solutions, *the close is theirs and that close should be expected!* The problem most salespeople run into is that they feel they're adequate in all areas of the sale except the close. For some reason, they "freeze" and develop a monumental stumbling block.

But back to the idea of showpersonship, that extra flair I talked about is the missing link that separates the average salesperson from the superstar. Showpersonship did not make an attorney like *F. Lee Bailey* a better technician, but I'm sure a lot richer and more highly regarded than a thousand attorneys who decorate the yellow pages. Showpersonship does not make an individual like *Billy Graham* more religious than some of our most pious, zealous and devoted clergy, but it certainly increases his congregation and extends his mission and goals in touching people around the world. Showpersonship does not make an individual like *Barbara Jordan* a better politician than others, but it increases the response to her proposals whether small or large. Showpersonship is that added genius or finesse that is not only possessed but developed through practice. It gives weight to what we say, and do, and separates us from the herd. The desired impression is "I am an individual, and reaching out; listen to what I have to say."

I'm not trying to steal away the necessity of a person's knowing his or her profession. Without a doubt we realize that today, one cannot be effective and meet the demand of the sophisticated markets, without knowing fully the technicalities of one's specific business. But beyond that requirement, there is another area which we must develop in order to perfect the quality of selling (and let's be realistic, we face selling in every part of our life and almost every day). No matter what our profession is, at one time or other, we're selling. Whether as a senior clerk who has to convince junior clerks of performing administrative tasks that are long and cumbersome, or the president of the company selling his Board of Directors a new program that he would like installed for his divisions, we're selling. If we tell our children we want them to take out the garbage and we'd like to have it done as soon as possible, we're selling. We're selling if we want our wife or girlfriend to pass on that overdue dinner or show, allowing us to watch a football game. We're selling if that state trooper has pulled us over after driving a little too fast. Selling enters everyone's life at any point and for a number of different reasons. But it is that motivated sale through *showpersonship* that makes the degree of success in selling, elevated or depressed in the final outcome.

One might ask how do you define *showpersonship?* What do you look for? What do you do to improve your showpersonship? Well, showpersonship is a very difficult quality to describe. Showpersonship shows more than flair and finesse. It shows *honesty, integrity, character, confidence, determination, resourcefulness, understanding, empathy, resolution,* and so forth. Alright, you say, now it's even worse. How can one develop so many ingredients to any great extent without involving himself in a project that would take a lifetime? Well, showpersonship is that extra natural ingredient that we should always keep in the back of our mind; it's not something developed through study on a day-to-day basis, for if studied daily, the actions stemming from that research will seem almost mechanical or unnatural. Rather, we should keep in mind that all verbal communication has meaning, particularly in selling. If it has meaning, it should be said with confidence, character and dignity, knowing that people search for a degree of involvement in our communication. I've said several times in the course of my management and selling career, particularly to several salespeople who have been under my tutelage, that all sales relate to *strategic conversation with a desired result!*

Many of our senior executives in major corporations throughout the world possess this quality without realizing it. They've reached the point in their careers where their conversations always have the desired results. Too often, regular conversation has no desired result, other than an exchange of ideas, but executives, being results-oriented, are always strategically handling their conversations in a way that achieves goals. So, too, is the aim of the salesperson. His or her conversation must achieve a result or all that transpired was an exchange of ideas, and no one is paid to just exchange ideas in the selling profession. It is ironic that most salespeople use that opening in acquiring an appointment for a sales interview; all they are looking for is to exchange a few ideas. If that becomes the case they, too, have lost sight of what their responsibilities are.

One of the best generalities to highlight showpersonship would be the communication of pride in what we do and what we are. Those salespeople who radiate pride in their own personal endeavors and the company they represent are the top producers. For virtually all true professionals, feeling a great deal of pride (not conceit) in their field, gives them confidence as well as self-satisfaction. It has been my experience in several sales situations, that when I carried myself with a degree of self-respect, while not compromising the reason for my sales call, the reaction was favorable, and I was given the floor with an open air and a more than subtle interest.

Observe any individual who portrays confidence. You automatically feel that the aura of his or her confidence must be real. This is a human quality common among all social beasts. Human beings feel more comfortable with strength and dedication to beliefs. We feel that believing strongly stimulates all the areas of worry and concern over mistakes. Surely one would not be so confident unless what he or she believed in was entirely true. Otherwise, they would be ignorant, naive or untrustworthy.

In most cases we tend to relate more to positive characteristic of a situation. There was an adage in the old Wild West days that if "one drew his gun he had better use it." If we consider the same analogy every time we open our mouths or make a point, that somewhere across us we face the long barrel of a six-shooter if we don't get it right, I think we might be stronger in our delivery. The best method to develop this feeling of showpersonship and pride is by establishing some principles, whether they be in sales, your personal dealings, in athletic events or any undertakings you may face. You must set those principles as guidelines; principles that cannot be compromised except for your own flexibility.

In dealing with the sales prospect allow that person enough room to control the buying, but not enough to control you. Never let a sales prospect make you wait for hours, or allow a prospect to treat your sales appointment as a nuisance. Don't be embarrassed by the premise that you are selling odds. Remember that our entire financial system is based upon sales and those individuals responsible for that function are the pillars of our economy. Never allow a prospect to intimidate you with his questions. By radiating self-respect with a calm and controlled attitude, you set the tone for your entire sales interview. Picture yourself and the prospect *passing a ball* to each other, while you're exchanging questions and answers. Picture that, in this instance, the prospect (with confidence) tosses the ball to you expecting you to fumble and drop it. This is the type of behavior many salespeople are confronted with. Try instead to relay a confident approach that takes the ball, looks at it and passes it back. This is the type of volley I relate to on a one-to-one relationship with a prospect.

I always picture juggling the ball and dropping it if I stutter in answering too quickly or poorly. Remember, if you toss the ball back, too high or too low, the prospect is liable to miss it. I have also learned that the questions I answer quickly are sometimes the ones to which I give the poorest answers. Again, this is the nature of the animal in sales. We feel obligated and pressured to respond with speed and confidence—but all too often that speed and confidence wind up to be an incorrect or fumbled reply. Remember that the *pause* after a question, to give you time to think before you answer, consists only of a matter of seconds and doesn't translate in reality to the vast gap it feels like at the time. The prospect would like to deal with a salesperson who puts thought into the words he or she delivers. The prospect would also like to feel that the answer he receives is tailored to his question and his question alone.

This is true with any situation. Consider parents who deal with children. All too often children receive quick and inadequately considered answers from their parents. This leaves them with the feeling that they do not deserve the time and interest of a considered answer. Children are smarter than most adults. Elements of showpersonship is even more evident to children. Children soon tire of the usual adult condescending attitude that makes them feel as if they're "non-persons." Adults who talk, listen and relate to the children's questions are the adults whom children most greatly endear. I am by no means a child psychologist. What I am saying is that all humans, whether young or old, prefer a well thought out, confident answer that reflects good faith.

This is true in sports as well. We've all seen less than total effort given to an athletic event that completely negates all the potential that the competing individual possesses. Paraphrasing the Old West analogy, don't draw your gun often, but when you do, make sure you use it and take good aim because that opportunity might not present itself again. If this is our approach (in general) with all the things we attack, we will steadily develop a more deliberate and confident action. Remember, showpersonship is a *class distinction*. So show a little *class* and people will notice.

Words of Wisdom for the Salesperson

- Every time I close a sale, I don't really celebrate—I just say to myself: *I just lost my best prospect.*

- I start my week with a Thursday—that way I don't lose any time on Monday morning planning where I'm going to go.

- I'm not productive *unless I'm in front of a buyer.* That's the critical measure in sales.

- I try to set aside one day a week for "trivial" stuff. That is, everything besides actually being in front of a buyer—including things such as follow-up phone calls, proposal writing, meetings with operations, etc.

- I consider the sales call to be like a 4-speed gear shift:

    - 1st—the approach or breaking the ice

    - 2nd—defining the problem

    - 3rd—presenting solutions

    - 4th—(high gear) the close

(Be smooth with these, as you would driving a car.)

- In approaching my prospect I work to eliminate the mental walls which separate us—build credibility, relax the prospect.

- If you really *listen* to the prospect, he'll give you all you need to write the successful proposal.

(These are adages and practices that have worked for me and many others. Internalize these phrases and ideas so that they become yours.)

5

Know It
or Forget It

Shortly after my service with the Marines, I acquired a job as a salesman, an insurance salesman to be more exact. I was only 20 years old, wide-eyed and anxious to learn. Fortunately, a trainer, or manager, played me a motivational tape, which indicated that surveys had proved that any individual who truly studied his or her chosen field or career for five years would become an expert in that area. Now it's important to remember that the film clarified this by saying that an individual had to be dedicated to learning about his or her field constantly for a period of *five years.* That is, *learn,* not merely participate or go through the motions. It further emphasized how, if an individual worked on a daily basis to acquire more knowledge—whether from written or other material relevant to that field—for a period of five years, they would most likely be the top contender in their field. It was at that time that I connected gaining an expertise in financial planning and selling insurance directly to making a large income for my family, and becoming wealthy. I made a pact with myself that for the first five years of my newly-chosen career, I would not allow myself the luxury of entertaining myself with reading material (such as books and courses) that dealt with matter not relevant to my success in insurance or finance. This might sound a bit extreme, and I have to tell you, most people cringe when I mention this point. I was told that I was starving the development of my total person, etc. Maybe that was true; but don't misunderstand me. I did go to movies and enjoy shows, but my *reading* time was very valuable; so I only allowed that time to be filled with what I treated as period of completing my education, obtaining my degree, and learning the world of insurance and finance.

I felt, and still feel, that that period of my life was a time when youthful ambition and anxiety were better used in paying my dues, earning my stripes, so to speak. My attitude was then, and still is, that although some success can be achieved at any age, it is best to develop one's personality toward success as soon as possible, particularly when an individual's energy and desire levels are highest, typically during their twenties and thirties. But the concept of becoming an expert in any field will never change. Five years of dedication in learning an area where you enjoy your success is more than enough time (if done diligently) to become an expert—the best!

We have the capacity as human beings to absorb and store more material than any computer in existence, but for some reason, it is difficult for us to pinpoint those specific practices and information that we utilize and retain. For that reason, I refer back to the title of this chapter *Know It or Forget It*. If the material that you are concentrating on is important enough to warrant your attention to achieve some form of success, by all means, *"know it."* If that material is unnecessary, irrelevant, wasteful or not directly connected to successful results, *"forget it."* As human computers, we must learn to dissect material. We must learn to ingest what is important and throw away what is unnecessary. Without this important skill, we endlessly undertake the torturous task of trying to relate and comprehend *everything* that seems minutely related to our field.

Most people will sign up at a local college for general interest courses, whether the general interest lies in Business, English, Skin Diving, or Aerobics. A general interest course is a great pursuit, if you are after general knowledge in a particular field, and learning the basics or key fundamentals. But my particular interest here lies in *specializing* the development of expertise in a *single* area that is important to you. I am not saying colleges suffer in supplying the education we need—relative to certain fields. But we are zeroing in on specialized development, so we must consider educational pursuits other than the traditional courses offered in colleges and universities, and explore the alternatives. For example: most industries provide adequate courses for your development in your field, whether it be banking, tool and die making, carpentry or hobbies such as weight lifting, running, or stamp collecting. Those fields or interests have their own courses, books, and magazines. Generally, the best way to get started in such self-help courses is to subscribe to one of their journals. That material will list additional materials that will help you to learn more, such as write-in courses, magazines that you can subscribe to, or books that you should purchase that relate to the materials and where they can be acquired. Of course, one of the richest resources for such information is the Internet. Often, simply performing a search on a major search engine, such as Google, Yahoo, or Ask Jeeves, and listing your area of interest, will provide a healthy list of resources, instruction, example, and often at little or no charge to you. Taking advantage of the wisdom and knowledge of those who have explored ahead of you is how you develop and grow.

You must become a human sponge so that you're constantly ingesting material that will make you an expert. Now you're probably picturing this poor soul sitting with piles of reading material stacked to the ceiling, so engrossed in accumulating information that life has no meaning except to learn. But don't be discouraged—we have more than enough hours in the day to read and ingest material without affecting our normal schedules or routines. How often do you find yourself waiting for a person, appointment, train, plane, bus or even at home in the bathroom? Sure, it's fine to occasionally read *Esquire, Cosmo, The Enquirer* or a new paperback, such as this one, but wouldn't it best serve your development to carry some material with you that will help you advance in your chosen career? How about the next time you're in the bathroom, carrying material other than jokes for the john, or when you're traveling, whether it be by train, plane, or as a passenger in a car? If you're not engrossed in conversation with the driver, the flight attendant or conductor, you have an excellent opportunity to read. Whatever works best for you. In fact, I've developed my own little formula that allows me a half an hour a day for the john (OK, all laughs aside), traveling, waiting, at night prior to sleeping and miscellaneous, totaling 2-½ hours a day or 17.5 hours a week to read. That is more than enough time to become well-developed or superior in our career or interests. Multiply 17.5 by 50 weeks for every year (allowing 2 weeks off for vacation) and you have *875 hours!* I'd like to point out here that I haven't allotted any extra time for weekends, holidays, or sick days, which means that the figure of 875 hours is conservative and probably low. Do you realize how much material can be consumed with 875 hours? *My God, even if you are a slow reader, you could read 100 books, 800 to 900 magazines or even listen to 800 cassettes,* all of which specialize in a particular endeavor. Important: Remember that I am talking about employing useful material while dissecting and cutting out the surplus and that which does not contribute to improving your skill. Certainly a person could stare at a magazine for hours, but I am sure he could read his usable material in about thirty minutes to an hour. Considering these components for just one year, can you imagine the profound affect this would have on your development over a period of five years? You would have over *4,000 hours* to become an expert or the equivalent of a *four-year college degree,* even a Masters Degree and credits to spare. (I am using a comparison of exact total study hours and direct classroom hours.)

My point is simple. If we want something badly enough, we can attain it without interrupting our lifestyle. This expression may be dated, but where there is a will, there's a way. First you must convince yourself that you want to control the situation. You can begin this by obtaining the kind of material that will help you advance and then applying it to those hours that are ideal for use. If you make a habit of doing this, it becomes compulsive. I've come to a point in my life where I can read at will and advance as far as I'd like to in those areas that are relevant.

Quite often we, as businessfolks, travel by plane. Certainly our schedules are demanding and time is of the essence. Have you ever stopped to consider the time you invest in going to the airport, setting up your delivery, handling security, waiting at a gate, getting in and out of the airport traffic and comparing that to travel by train? Again, I am not pitting one mode of travel against the other. Let me provide you with some insight into a little trip I recently made. About a month ago I had a business meeting in Syracuse. There is a local train station about six blocks from my house. I thought it would be interesting and relaxing to avoid the hustle and bustle of getting to the plane by taking the train instead. Several of the railroad companies today are providing excellent services at reasonable rates, accessible to wherever you live. I left at about 6 o'clock in the morning and arrived in Syracuse about 11 o'clock. A friend of mine left from the same area at about 7:30am and arrived somewhere around 10:30. I recall leisurely walking down to the train station, purchasing a round trip excursion ticket that cost in the neighborhood of $50, sitting in this comfortable train, napping for the first hour or two, reading for the next hour; then I strolled down to the dining car and had a pleasant lunch as the train arrived in Syracuse. It happened to be one of the most relaxing, enjoyable trips I've made in a long time, and I accomplished a lot. In the round-trip analysis, I found that I had read almost an entire book that was important to a project I'm involved in, completed several of my company's administrative responsibilities, ate and slept.

Now let's get back to my friend who saved all that traveling time by leaving at 7:30am and arriving at 10:30. I forgot to mention that he left home at about 5:30 in the morning to beat the traffic and get into the airport and get his baggage on board. He also was delayed at the airport an extra hour and fifteen minutes after his arrival because of delays with security and checkout. So in total, he really did leave at about 5:30 and arrived, for practical purposes, at about the same time I did. Not really much difference in time at all between the two modes of travel. But there *were* some other differences. He certainly didn't sleep at all. Other than browsing an airline magazine, he didn't read at all and the first thing he mentioned when we saw each other was that he was starving. End result: I was more relaxed and in a better frame of mind for my business meeting, had most of the projects and reading material covered prior to arrival, and had a head start on the administrative responsibilities that were facing me the next day. Oh, by the way, I also saved myself (rather my company) well over $90 in round-trip fare, not to mention incidentals. Apply that factor once a month, you've saved over $1,000 each year, while putting more valuable time back in your schedule. Result: You accomplish more. Again, I am sure there are instances where taking a plane will provide you more time, such as traveling coast to coast, and I certainly do use a plane when necessary, but in this day and age of jet traffic and airport security, let's give a little credit back to the railroad, too.

These are some of the small areas in which we can improve our expertise. Remember, becoming a success at anything is not a small job; it entails work, study and self-management. And a little imagination goes a long way. I'm sure you can add to my ideas and plug in those extra hours where you normally think to yourself, wow, what a wasted day, or what a wasted night—what did I get accomplished? Well, if you add a little more knowledge to something that you're really looking to succeed in, then you *have* accomplished something. Remember, *"Knowledge is power."*

6

A Blueprint and Outline for Careers

Your Place in the Job Market

Choosing the Right Position and Company.

    a.   Self analysis

    b.   Appearance—dress, grooming

    c.   Research—company nationally and locally

    d.   Resume—professional and to the point

    e.   Confidence—but not arrogance

    f.   Enthusiasm

    g.   Strength—don't over-compromise

    h.   Flexibility—able to do anything

    i.   Stability

    j.   Ambitious—but not ruthless

Starting and Maintaining Your Position

1.   Establish Goals Early—Business and Personal

    a.   Dream, real and minimum

    b.   Where do you want to be in 6 months, 1 year, 3 years, 5 years, etc.?

    c.   What price will you pay?

        1.   Hours

        2.   Loyalty

        3.   Study!!!!!

        4.   Principles

        5.   Goals

    d.   How many times can you bounce back?

2.   Find a symbol, leader, someone of stature, success, and accomplishments to learn from, regardless of whether the person is alive or dead, known or unknown. Study their good points, undertakings that brought about their success, and learn, don't copy. You'll find they all have common qualities.

3.   Read motivational literature, not downers, avoid downer people.

* Use this as a checklist when analyzing your career or when preparing for a new one.

The Everyday Job in Itself—Do's and Don'ts

1. Expect efficiency, never give excuses.

2. Give the little extra.

3. Try to know something about all the jobs connected to or with yours. You never can tell, someday you may be supervising them or changing. If you can change or learn easily, you're never without a position.

4. Work late if necessary. Don't believe it doesn't pay to volunteer for extra work; that kind of thinking is food for failure. Don't make an issue of your extra work, it very seldom goes unnoticed.

5. Be involved with your office and its success, don't have an "I don't care attitude." The day might come when your office won't care about you.

6. Once you're starting to prove yourself, casually let your worthwhile goals get to the right people. It might be the fuse that propels you into management or greater opportunity. Sometimes executives can't see the forest for the trees, a little coaxing always helps (if you're worth it).

7. Don't be overly involved in office politics, and don't take sides. Be honest and fair but never overly committed; you might stick your neck out too far. Remember executives are like dynasties, some die out.

8. Always believe in yourself. If you're right, you're right, and that's all there is to it.

9. Avoid lateness, sloppy dress, absenteeism, excuses and more excuses.

7

Recommended Reading

Recommended Reading

1. *Psycho Cybernetics*-Maxwell Maltz

2. *Dress For Success*-John T. Malloy

3. *How To Get More Done In Less Time*-Joseph Cooper

4. *Formula For Success*-Lawrence Appley

5. *Success Through A Positive Mental Attitude*-Clement Stone

6. *How I Raised Myself from Failure to Success in Selling*-Frank Betcher

7. *Winning Through Intimidation*-Robert Ringer

8. *Power*-Michael Korda

9. *How To Develop a Super Memory*-Harry Lorayne

10. *Body Language*-Julius Fast

11. *You Can Work Your Own Miracles*-Napoleon Hill

12. *Think and Grow Rich*-Napoleon Hill

13. *Live For Success*-John T. Malloy

14. *Power Speaking That Gets Results*-Glen "Tiger" Ellison

15. *Say What You Mean*-Rudolph Flesch

16. *The Art of Conversation*-James Morris

17. *Unmasking the Face*-Frieson

18. *The Management of Time*-James T. McCay

19. *Word Power Made Easy*-Norman Lewis

20. *Contact—The First Four Minutes*-Leonard Zuner, M.D.

21. *Personnel*-Strauss & Sayler

22. *Faster Reading Self Taught*-Harry Shifter

23. *Personal Vitality*-Donald Miller

24. *Everybody's Business*-Milton Moskowitz

25. *Success—Pure & Simple*-Dominic Certo

Part II
Sports

The Author and Sports

Dom featured in a *Muscle World* magazine summer 1981.

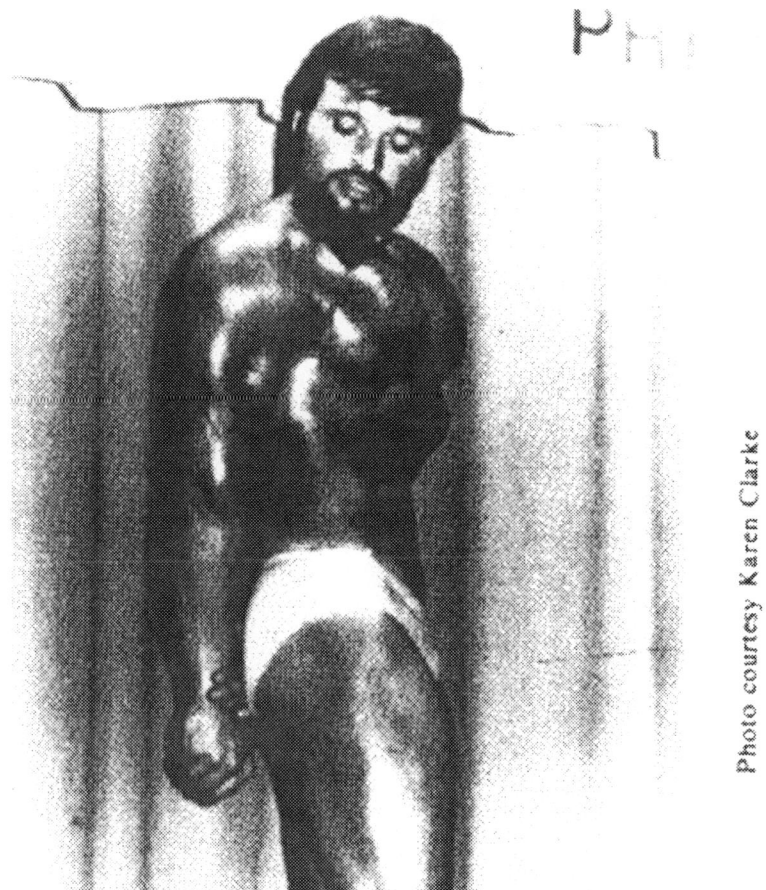

Dom in the 1976 Mr. North America competition medium class.

Photo courtesy *Armed Forces Press*

Certo in the 1968 Atlantic Armed Forces track championships—Guantanamo, Cuba—100 yd. dash winner.

Courtesy *Marine News* and *Leatherneck* magazine

"Kid Certo" 1968, (age 17) Fleet Marine Division & Regimental boxing champion. Dom appears in the film Pumping Iron II and on several TV talk show.

1976 Mr. & Ms. Eastern America. Here the author presents awards as promoter and IFBB official.

"OLD TIMERS PRO DAY"

| G. Raymond | JOE DIMAGGIO (Baseball) | Joe Fuoco (Attorney) | G. Pryor (bowling) | DOM CERTO (bodybuilding) | WILLIE MAYS (Baseball) |

The author with Willie Mays (far right) & Joe DiMaggio (2nd from the left).

8

Sports

Every one of us at one time or another has cheered an athlete to victory, whether it be the heavyweight boxing champion fighting to regain his title, the Olympic runner pushing desperately against immeasurable odds, or the running back, sprinting for a touchdown. Even the most sedate person at one time or another has felt the anxiety of competition and exhilaration of triumph as a spectator or competitor himself.

What is this fascination with sports and athletics? What is this beckoning of competition that touches almost every man, woman, and child? The fact is that the human being is a competitor and rival by instinct. Culture and technology will never rob men of their most basic impulse to challenge each other in the arena, on stage, or the playing field. By Divine fate, we are bestowed with a mind, body and soul. Some of us, through a master plan, have been given more talent, ability and resources to prevail in sports, some have been given an even greater gift—desire! I certainly agree that it is a pleasure to watch someone who is naturally blessed with the ability, grace and substance to make difficult and demanding events seem almost comfortable and carefree. They are the wonders of our age and a beauty to behold, but for all that art, one can't help but quicken for the underdog. Everyone is quieted by the individual who, with no more than anyone else, grinds, fights, and pushes his way to the top. That person is our alter ego. That person represents the soul inside each one of us. Sure we watch with wonder the blessed ones, and gifted people who meet the rigors, demands, and obstacles of their sports. But the rough-edged, plain 'Jane' or 'Jim' who goes for it all and reaches deep down inside is our true hero, for we all have that fire within us.

In 1968 I trained furiously for our Olympic trials. I had amassed enough points in my sport to qualify for Nationals based on an elimination system between fighters. Boxing in the Special Services offered some privileges, but we still had normal duties. As a youth of 18 years, I was overcome with the desire to win a Gold Medal but I had to remember to qualify first. My only competition at the time was a young black athlete, my age, from Kentucky. He was underrated and that has nothing to do with this story except for the fact that he had a burning desire to just be good enough to make the team. Qualifying, for me, seemed inevitable. This particular athlete was behind me in points and matches and I didn't expect any challenge. Further, his schedule was more demanding than mine during elimination bouts, making it harder for him to catch up for a match with me. Meanwhile, I was still having visions of Gold Medals and fame until the day came when I met up with this individual. I still wasn't worried. Everyone assured me that he was scared, and the local sports people favored me anyway. I stayed cocky until the bell rang and we were well into the first round. This athlete fought furiously and with incredible accuracy. He never let up. I felt that I was a spectator until later in the fight when I realized I needed points and gave it all I had to catch up. We bloodied each other terribly, and our eyes were bloated to the point of obscenity. When the fight ended, we collapsed on each other. The judges announced it was a split decision with the young black man winning by one point.

I was shocked, overcome and distraught. I could stand up straight and stared, watching the other fighter being carried out, but he had triumphed. He was the conqueror! He had reached for that moment and had given it all he had. Though he was spent, he was satisfied. I felt I could have given more, but it was too late. Suddenly the Gold Medal disappeared and so did my dream. There is a lesson to be learned from this. One must take each step carefully before he or she leaps. Sometimes visions of grandeur become overwhelming, but we must win each small battle in order to win a war. That black athlete went on to compete and win a medal (not gold but a medal) and I went back overseas.

As a judge for world professional athletic events, I was often asked what I found to be common among the greatest champions. Having been an official in boxing, track, bodybuilding, and weightlifting, I found that the ingredients and characteristics are typically the same; overwhelming desire, a single-mindedness of purpose, self-respect, and attitude. Heaven help the gifted athlete who has a slight edge over a challenger with a strong attitude, determination and passion to win. The bodybuilding competitors do not meet with the same type of urgency on contest day to fight as furiously and win. *There, the results of years of work (generally) will produce a champion.* But those ingredients I mentioned can work for the bodybuilder also during his training period, when he really competes against his rivals. This is true in track and other singular sports, where passion and determination must propel the athlete during his training to give him the edge over what might be a more gifted athlete.

In 1983, Chris Dickerson, a small black man from New York City, went on to defeat men from all over the world in the most coveted bodybuilding event created, the Mr. Olympia. He also was the first black Mr. America. Chris stood about 5 feet 4 inches and was constantly criticized by some bodybuilding experts as having short arms, weak joints, and slight features in general. They would write about how it was impossible for someone of his size to compete effectively against the giants and hulks in the sport, but Chris did, and Chris won. Not only the Mr. Olympia, but Mr. Universe, Mr. America and Grand Prix Pro Tour. He is a determined man filled with a passion, a good attitude, grace, and integrity. He was a pleasure to watch and judge. He put everything into each event and fought to win. He is a true competitor. He didn't always talk about the next competition or the next show. He would relentlessly track what is *now*, and this must be true with all of us.

In 1975 and 1976 I competed nationally in bodybuilding events and had the good fortune to appear on the same stage with Arnold Schwarzenegger. Although Arnold was just guest posing and not in his best shape, he exhibited every quality of a champion in his smile, intensity and purpose. He provided the fans with entertainment and excitement. When I scurried backstage during breaks to force out push-ups and pumps for a better appearance, Arnold commented that all that extra exercise and preparation has to be done long before the contest day. How right he was.

We all must prepare for our events whatever they may be. It demands work, day in and out, adherence to diet, sleep, and increased performance. We must continually improve and tax the body more, as it adjusts, or the body becomes indifferent and even more difficult. The body, like the mind, has an instinctive will to improve, learn more, and experience more. If it is neglected or ignored it reacts with poor performance.

Good athletes set goals, which is a common feature in all three sections of this book. Without goals we drift and kid ourselves. Get into the habit, whatever your sport is: running, boxing, football, bodybuilding or basketball, to record your progress and to ledger your diet and gains. Read inspirational material, go to events, write for courses and believe in yourself. Try to be a little stronger every day, particularly in the mind, because the mind will ultimately rule the body, determining success or failure. Realize that many champions might have had less natural abilities than you, but great wells of burning desire and a good attitude. It's basic and commonplace, but reach down inside and have some guts; you'll find you probably have more than you expected.

Joseph Weider

(Publisher, Businessman, Athlete and Author)
Woodland Hills, California

Joe Weider as a young champion athlete and trainer.

In 1947, Joe Weider moved from Canada to the U.S.A., establishing offices in Jersey City and New York. He worked from these headquarters until 1973. In that year, the U.S.A. headquarters was moved to Woodland Hills, California under the name of Weider Health & Fitness. This has become a mecca for people all over the world. Athletes and bodybuilders, strength and conditioning coaches, exercise and nutritional experts from everywhere, all come seeking Joe Weider's advice. Life Magazine *has said bodybuilding, health, nutrition and exercise was the business of the 1980s. Forty-five years before that, Joe Weider was saying the same thing and started a movement that has now come to be recognized as the most dynamic business in the world today. The* Wall Street Journal, *in a January 1983 article by Charles Garfield, President of Peak Performance Center, named Joseph Weider and his brother Ben as two of the leading and most successful executives in the world of business.*

Joe Weider takes all of this acclaim in stride. After all, he has known all along, since that day back in 1939 when he wrote the articles for his first magazine *Physique,* that his dreams, his concepts, his systems, would become reality. It took 45 years of hard work, patience, and dedication, for the world to understand and now follow his methods of physical training and food supplementation. But, one would not expect less from Joe Weider, his mark on sports will be well documented when the comprehensive history of sports is finally written.

Joe Weider could easily fall into any category of this book for his outstanding success in business, sports and the arts, but because of his tremendous assistance to thousands of athletes, millions of fans and readers, and his advancement of a very popular sport around the world, we, the publishers and author, felt his place appropriate in this section.

Joe Weider was born in Montreal, Canada in 1922. He was always involved in sports, and was an outstanding wrestler and champion weight-lifter during his school years.

Joe Weider today.

He started *Your Physique Magazine* in 1939, at the age of seventeen. *Physique* is a magazine dealing with bodybuilding and strength conditioning as well as nutrition. It was apparent at a very early age that Joe Weider had dreams he intended to turn into reality. He's done that and more. Joe Weider was a pioneer, using bodybuilding and food supplementation as a preparation for sports training. Before anyone else had the concept of producing foods in concentrated forms for athletic performance, Joe Weider developed protein and vital amino acids as a supplement to the diet of athletes and those involved in training and stress situations. In 1946 he and his brother, Ben Weider, formed the *International Federation of Body Building (IFBB)*. This organization was dedicated to the creation of a world bodybuilding movement. The IFBB promoted strength conditioning for athletes. The results of its training and nutritional methods have been well documented and the Weider Company has modified these methods and programs to fit the needs of the general public for optimal living. Through the years, the IFBB has developed into a federation of 120 nations and is one of the strongest sport groups in the world today.

The IFBB publishes medical and technical research and provides this information free of charge to national Olympic committees throughout the world. Leaders of national sports federations and training coaches from around the world all look to the IFBB and the Weider total training system for guidance and inspiration. The motto of the IFBB created by Joe Weider is "Bodybuilding is Important For Nation Building." His motto is just a small part of the Joe Weider philosophy followed by millions of young and active older people who, for the past 65 years have followed Joe Weider avidly. In 1947, Joe Weider pioneered food supplementation in protein form, and has, since that time, created a line of protein, weight gain, weight loss, and muscle building products that are the leaders in their fields in the U.S.A. and the world. These products are used and endorsed by leading bodybuilders and athletes who, along with strenuous physical activity, make food a part of their training. Weider food supplements are Number One among athletes in the world today.

In the years following, 1939 *Your Physique Magazine,* grew in popularity and circulation, changed in name to *Muscle Power, Muscle Builder,* and is now known as *Muscle & Fitness. Muscle & Fitness* is regarded as being the most popular bodybuilding and strength training magazine in the U.S.A. today, reaching over *1,700,000 readers* every month. In addition to the English version sold and read in the U.S.A., Canada and England, it is also published in Germany, Italy, Sweden, Finland and in Arabic for Egypt and Lebanon and shortly will be printed in Japan.

Joe Weider also created and publishes *Shape Magazine,* which is dedicated to women who are interested in optimal health and physical appearance. *Shape* is now the number one women's magazine of its kind in America and the world today. Monthly circulation recently reached 570,000 copies per month. Close to 1,750,000 readers closely follow every months issue for its expert advice on diet, nutrition and exercise. *Shape* is a women's magazine with a woman editor and staff. They deal with women's lives and responsibilities. The third magazine, titled *Flex,* has just been published with the specific goal of developing hard core bodybuilding to develop the sport to its logical conclusion. Career opportunities—How to make a living while training, and after one retires. It also brings to the bodybuilder, information on body building from around the world.

In a tribute to his creativity in the field of publishing, Joe Weider was named Publisher of the Year in 1983 by the Periodical and Book Association of America. A luncheon in his honor was held at the Helmsley Palace Hotel in New York City, attended by over 200 publishers from throughout North America—a long way from that day in Montreal at the age of 17, when he started his first magazine. Joe Weider is known throughout the world as a trainer of champions. His methods are used by athletes in all sports who continually consult with him for his expertise.

In 1965, Joe Weider envisioned and created the Mr. Olympia Professional Bodybuilding Contest. This contest was instrumental in expanding international interest in the sport of bodybuilding. In 1965, a prize of $1,000 was given to the winner of the first Mr. Olympia Contest. In 1984, the prize was $100,000, just a small indication of the growth of this sport over that short span of time.

Joe Weider is the creator and developer of the Weider Health and Fitness System. Due to Joe Weider's pioneering efforts, food supplementation and exercise is recognized as the necessary foundation for both physical and mental health throughout the athletic world today. More and more ordinary people are coming to realize the importance of food, vitamin, mineral supplementation and exercise to enhance their lives.

Joe Weider's Personal Statement:

"The Key to Success is to read biographies on how others succeeded. Invariably you will find success is based on confidence, awareness and perseverance.

The key to success is to also believe in yourself and your plans. You will encounter some set-backs along the way, but sometimes it is necessary to take a step backwards, to move two steps forward.

I started working when I was twelve years old and my goal was to get bodybuilding accepted amongst sportsmen, the medical profession, and to create a sport from bodybuilding itself. I have achieved all these goals through determination, because I believed in what I was promoting. These same principles can be applied for the ultimate success of any acceptable program.

Work should be fun and one must derive pleasure out of it as otherwise you will be defeated before you start.

Perseverance will guarantee success."

Michael Bergius Katz

(Mr. Universe—Former New York Jets Offensive Guard)
New Haven, Connecticut

Mike Katz as a N.Y. Jet.

All-American, All-State Football, Hamden High School
All-New England Hockey—Hamden High
All-District Track & Field—Hamden High

All-League Fullback—Southern Connecticut State University
New York Jets—Offensive Guard 1966-67
Mr. Teenage Connecticut—1963
Mr. Teenage America 4th—1965
Mr. Connecticut—1966
Mr. New England—1967
Mr. East Coast—1967
Mr. Junior America—1968
Mr. America (Runner-up)—1969
Mr. America—1970
Mr. World—1972
Mr. Universe—1972
Mr. Olympia (Runner-up)—1976
Mr. Olympia (Competitor)—1981

Business Experience:
1979-1981 Product Development/Marketing,
Lecturer Seyforth and Futuron Ind.
(Nutritional supplements)
1981-Present President of World Gym
East & Woman's Fitness World
1982 President/Creator of Mike Katz
Commercial Equip. Co. Div. of
Wallingford Barbell.

Marital Status: Married
Children: Michael, 12 & Michele, 10
Education: Southern Conn. State Univ.
B.S. Health & Physical Educ. 1966
M.A. Health & Physical Educ. 1970
Doctoral Program: Administration &
Supervision currently

Present Employment: Hamden Board of Education Health Education Teacher for 17
years

Mike Katz as a bodybuilder.

"As a young boy I had dreams like most to be 'famous, something special, out-standing at something, one of a kind, different and unique from others' and ultimately that became what I lived my life by.

At the time my interest was in the area of athletics probably due in fact to my father's keen background in sports. His subtle but supportive attitude in that area would go on to have a lasting effect on my future successes. He would say things like, 'give it your best,' 'don't ever be a quitter,' and 'strive always to improve.' I loved and respected him and learned to make those words the hallmark I in turn lived by.

I have to say it was much more than just hard work that enabled me to succeed. For me it was a blind and totally unending dedication to achieve the goals I had set forth. The greatest obstacles one usually must overcome is their own lack of confidence and a totally positive attitude. For me that was never a problem. It was the negative 'stuff from jealous, envious, and bigoted people that fueled my fires within. 'Their doubts turned into my deeds.'

Another problem one must overcome is the self-sacrifice it takes to accomplish a given goal. At least, that is what those on the outside looking in believe. Again that was no problem. I believe once the word sacrifice is thought of, or admitted to, the chance of success becomes if not impossible, at least remote.

I believe it is impossible to neatly separate my life's accomplishments into separate units. My success as a World Champion Bodybuilder can be attributed to those qualities that motivated me to be a professional football player, successful businessman, teacher, parent, and most important of all, a 'human being.'"

Lori Bowen

(Champion Bodybuilder)
San Antonio, Texas

Born in Dallas, Texas, lived there until high school graduation in 1976. Moved to San Antonio. Lori became interested in bodybuilding after attending the Mr. San Antonio in 1981. Miss Bowen entered her first contest in 1981 and has won numerous titles since. Her titles include:

AFWB American and USA Champion-1983
Miss Turner, Texas-1976
Miss Texas-1982
South Central USA Champion-1983
and several other place titles
in 1983.

Lori was a cheerleader through high school and worked at several odd jobs while training vigorously for her well-deserved titles. She was featured in the movie "Pumping Iron 11." Here are some of her comments:

"I never realized what I had the ability to do until I actually started training, then the more I learned the more I internalized the sport, the more I wanted to improve. I think the main thing to remember is that you have to want to do it. You have to decide if it is worth the sacrifice and hard work; be blessed with the right ingredients; so to waste them would be foolish. I feel any young man or woman attempting to succeed at a chosen sport must list their desires and plan to get there. I intend to go on to more and greater challenges, a business career, modeling, perhaps even acting or movies. Whatever the goal I will work for it and follow good instinct."

Bill Pearl

(World Champion Bodybuilder-Businessman-Author)
Pasadena, California

Mr. America—1953
Mr. Universe—1953
Mr. USA—1956
Mr. Universe—1961
Mr. Universe—1967
Mr. Universe—1971
WBBG Hall of Fame—1978
IFBB National Chairman of the Professional Physique
Judges Committee.

Bill Pearl has personally trained more physique champions than anyone in the sport. He has operated his own health clubs and business concerns since 1954. Bill is a credit to the sport and success in general. Here are his words:

"Success has been accomplished by having myself, as well as those I worked with, use the same formula that has always worked for me: keeping a positive attitude, *setting goals,* following personalized training programs, keeping accurate records and *seeking advice from the best."*

Carla Dunlap

(World Champion Bodybuilder-Swimmer)
Irvington, New Jersey

Carla Dunlap, September 1980.

Current Major Bodybuilding Titles:
1983 Miss Olympia (IFBB)
A FWB American Women's Champion
1981 and 1982 (amateur) IFBB Pro World Women's Champion—1983 IFBB Pro
Team Champion USA—1982

Swimming Awards:

1978 Bronze Medal in the Inaugural
Olympic National Sports Festival
1977 Junior National Indoor Champion
Cygnets of San Antonio, Texas

Carla also appears on the cover.

"Born October 22, 1954 and raised in Newark, New Jersey, I grew up the next youngest daughter in a family of four sisters and a brother. Talk about competitive beginnings! My childhood was middle class, happy and full of exposure to anything and everything—cultural, classical, people, places, education and self-knowledge. My educational trek began as a kindergarten drop-out (we moved and I was left mid-stream, too far away to finish the old school and too late to start the new school), proceeded to fifth grade truancy due to brilliance and too much boredom which fortunately led me to being advanced one grade and finally ended (or continued) with passing an exam and gaining entry into the prestigious Newark Arts High School as a commercial arts major at the ripe old age of 12 years. My schooling culminated in a full scholarship to the Newark School of Fine and Industrial Arts, graduating in 1974 with a diploma in Advertising Design. With special permission papers from the Board of Education, I began to work at the age of 14 as a summer counselor with the Newark YWCA. I continued working as head counselor, life guard, water instructor, warehouse distributor, sales girl, office clerk, hard and soft line layout artist, Associate Physical Director (San Antonio, Texas YMCA), and finally back in New York as a sales assistant with Shearson/American Express.

Carla Dunlap relaxed.

Only three things mattered to me growing up. A consuming passion to perform in the physical sense, the need and talent to express and communicate through the practical and performing arts, and a healthy competitive spirit. Of the three, the first and last won out. Throughout high school and college I danced in a road troupe, taught and took classes in dance and gymnastics, learned to swim and ultimately competed in gymnastics, speed swimming and synchronized swimming. While competing in synchro, I swam for teams in New Jersey, New York, California and Texas. During my tenure with the Cygnets of San Antonio, Texas, we became the 1977 Junior National Indoor Team champions and participated in the Inaugural Olympic National Sports Festival in 1978 and again in 1979, winning the bronze medal in the team event for "Team South" in 1978.

Bodybuilding found me through an introduction by Steve Wennerstrom, now the official IFBB Women's Historian. On a lark with just a swimmers physique, I entered what was to be a landmark contest, held in Warminster, Pennsylvania in

August of 1979. It was a classic case of being in the right place at the right time. The Wave of Bodybuilding for Women began to rise from that point forward and myself along with a handful of other women have been riding the crest ever since.

If I had to share a word of encouragement with the world about the way to success, it would be: 'Don't ever be afraid to go after your dreams or take a risk, because basically the biggest obstacle you'll ever encounter is yourself.' I used to worry as a teen that I didn't have an 'important' direction like everyone else. That I should be going the way everyone else was—a secretary, a banker, something with a very standard badge of achievement. But I always came full circle—back to the physical. You can only deny your natural direction for so long. It may not always lead to outstanding financial success, but then in my book, healthy and happy have always come before wealthy.

My parents never told me there were places I couldn't go, nor things I couldn't do."

Clarence Bass

(World Champion Athlete—Businessman—Author)
Albuquerque, New Mexico

In 1962, he graduated from the University of New Mexico School of Law, ranked second in his class. He practiced law in Albuquerque, New Mexico since then, first as an associate and then a partner in a well-known law firm, and since 1973 as a sole practitioner. He now practices mainly in the areas of real estate and family law.

In the sports field, he won his first major award in 1954 when he became the New Mexico High School Pentathlon champion, a five-event contest made up of push-ups, chin ups, jump reach, bar vault, and 300-yard shuttle run. A year later he became the Albuquerque and New Mexico Olympic Lifting Champion and then won various regional contests, including the Southwest and Rocky Mountain Championships. He placed second in the National Teenage Championship and in the Junior National Weight lifting Championship.

His most recent success has been in bodybuilding, where he won Mr. America Past 40 *and* Mr. U.S.A. Past 40 (Short Class) *titles in 1978 and 1979; in the latter contest he won the Best Abdominals, Best Legs and Most Muscular awards. In the course of preparing for these contests he reduced his body fat to 2.4 percent. (Top marathoners like Alberto Salazar carry around 6 percent body fat). He wrote and published two successful books,* Ripped *and* Ripped 2, *which detail his diet and training methods. His question and answer column,* The Ripped Department, *appears monthly in* Muscle & Fitness Magazine.

In addition, he is a national and international physique judge, and vice president of the National Physique Committee of the U.S.A. Clarence is married and has one son.

"Success and happiness come from taking control of your life. As a lawyer, I've found greater satisfaction in being a sole practitioner than a partner in a large law firm. In my own office, I can handle the cases I enjoy and I'm not pressured to practice in areas that I find unpleasant. In addition, I can structure my day to allow time to pursue my bodybuilding interests.

Needless to say, it took some luck and a lot of effort to put myself in the position I now enjoy. The secret, I think, lies in doing the best you can in whatever you undertake. If something is worth doing, it's worth doing right. However, we all have strengths and weaknesses. As you go through life, it's important to decide what you enjoy and do well. Don't beat your head up against the wall trying to do something for which you aren't suited. Decide what you like to do and do best, and then, do it for all you're worth."

James J. Osborne

(Pro-Football Referee)
Erdenheim, Pennsylvania

NFL line judge (referee—professional football)
Former Intercollegiate football judge and referee
High school All-American
Graduate (football scholarship) of
Villanova University in 1960 with an
outstanding four-year playing record.
Former vice-president of a large textile company, currently a sales executive with a large service corporation when not refereeing.

"For a person to work up the ladder of success in football he must pay the price of consistent playing progress from high school through college and so on. He or she must make a continual vertical move avoiding many other past times to become the best at their position. As you gain experience, try other positions to gain perspective for the sport but build your strengths. Remember, in football you're working with many different personalities and my suggestion is to be yourself, not striving for perfection, but damn close to it. Gather the best from all these different individuals so as to develop yourself better. Be like a duck, 'calm on the outside while peddling like hell underneath.' Know the game inside and out, realize it is played for the benefit of others also, use discretion and common sense. As an official, I've found there are many critics and negatives so I often refer to Teddy Roosevelt's statements:

> "It is not the critic who counts; not the man who points out how the strong man stumbled or where the doer of deeds could have done it better, the credit belongs to the man who is actually in the arena, whose face is marred by dust and sweat and blood; who strives valiantly; who errors and comes short again and again because there is no effort without error and shortcomings; but he who does actually strive to do the deeds; who knows the great enthusiasm, the great devotion; who spends himself in a worthy cause; who at the best knows in the end the triumph of high achievement and who at the worst, if he fails, at least failed while doing greatly, so that his place shall never be with those cold and timid souls who know neither victory, nor defeat."

—"Get into the arena and strive valiantly to climb to the top of the ladder."

9

Competitive Spirit

"I Dare You!" Oh, how that raises our anxiety level. Those few words bring out the competitive spirit we all have—how can we forget how those words rang so clear as children. *I dare you!* And what was our usual reaction as a child? Well, long before society and the evolution of growing up tempered our attitudes, our most immediate reaction was to accept the dare—stomp it into the ground, not vindictively, but with a healthy, confident energy level that meant we were going to try. Why should it change now? Why should a person feel intimidated by competition?

Earlier, I mentioned to you that George Bernard Shaw stated life was a state of mind. Let's apply that formula to this particular theme. Competition can be used to your best advantage or disadvantage, depending on your state of mind. **The state of mind that you revel in or suffer with (when competition enters the picture) is based upon the setting and attitude you first create.**

Let's present some examples: You're a pretty fair golfer and you pride yourself on a good drive. Usually you step up to the tee, hold your club with complete authority and *wham!* The ball soars straight and true every time for at least 200 yards. But suddenly, you play head-on with another golfer, whom you respect. He says, "Let's lay a little money on it. I bet you can't do it." Well, you're the same golfer, nothing's changed. It's the same golf ball and the same club. Your vision hasn't suddenly fogged, your health is as good as always, but suddenly you say to yourself, "Damn, now is when I'll probably blow it," or "What did he have to go and bet for?" or, "I'm good, I can do it—am I good?" It's not really important what the exact wording is, but it all boils down to the same thing. *You're setting yourself up for failure.* You are creating with your state of mind the outcome that the individual who's betting against you wants.

Let's make another example: You're an excellent salesman; you work hard at your job. Every day you practice new and better methods of communicating with your prospect. You make a good living—do a good job. You're respected by your superiors and you have the potential for being more than just an average-to-good salesman. Then one day your boss or sales manager announces that a sales contest will begin and Joe, Harry, Pete, Bill, Tom, or the entire sales force will be competing against each other for the valued prize of a trip to Bermuda. Now what are your thoughts? Are your thoughts, "Hey, great prize. *I think I'll win it.*" No, that would be thinking positively and the pressure has just been applied so more likely your thoughts center around, *"Damn, couldn't they have a contest when I was going good all year? Do they have to have it now? There probably isn't a piece of business to be had."* Is this a way of making an excuse for yourself to take the pressure off? It sure sounds like it. Or just the opposite approach. *"Damn, I've been going good so far. Now it's their turn. Probably Tom or Harry is going to start to hit it big. I'm sure they'll beat me out"* or even, *"Wow, there're 500 people in the sales force. I haven't a chance in hell of beating out all those people."* Gee, aren't those thoughts all too common? I'll give you one more example before we attack this little problem that we all occasionally suffer.

This time we'll spread the anxiety level around a little bit to include a group of people. Your football team has been having a fair-to-good season; things have been starting to improve. Your defense has been plugging the holes and your offense has been gaining more and more yardage. You all get a little cocky and brag about how good you are and how you are just as good as the regional champs. Pretty soon they'll be easy pickings. Finally, the day comes that you play those regional champs and you are playing great. You suddenly have a two-touchdown lead. Their defense seems to be demolished, but a little bit of doubt starts to grow and radiate. Even worse, the thought suddenly comes to mind that this is a championship team you're playing. Yet by some bit of luck, you're two touchdowns ahead. It's impossible! How can you win? Your luck's got to run out sometime. Maybe it's just one player thinking that thought, and he happens to be your receiver on the next play and when the ball is passed, he doesn't catch it. Then that tight end who walks in with them starts to sense that same doubt as he looks in his teammate's face and sees the look of defeat; then he starts to play below par and so on with the quarterback and the line and then what do you see happen? We've all seen it—a healthy well-playing, underdog team collapses after they establish a little bit of a lead over a known championship team. At first they have all the ingredients to beat that team, so why the change in game plan? Well, those are just a few of the "situation comedies" that all too often are not that funny, because failures can lead to disasters and disasters to failures in our own positive development.

Okay, we agree with this. We all see this problem and we all know that we occasionally are faced with this kind of mental attitude. So how do we correct it? First of all there's some degree of luck involved with everything. But most things that we accomplish (particularly when the result comes from our direct actions) stem from skill or our control over the situation. Our control and expertise is even more evident in situations where we consistently perform to a certain level, but fail when the slightest pressure is presented. So how about taking the attitude, *"Am I the victim of stupidity? Am I going to let this little bit of pressure change me and what I am? Am I to be made a fool? Do I control my life? Should I be led about like sheep?"* Or even better, how about, *"I know that I'm good at this and I've been doing well so I don't think I'll change. As a matter of fact, this bet or prize will make my results even sweeter."* Or for the very confident individual, how about trying, *"Boy, what a turkey, giving me an opportunity to do what I always wanted to do, with a prize besides. They ought to have their heads examined. Hell, I'll take their prize or their money. After all, that's what life's all about, getting ahead."*

You see, **once we start to form a success pattern in our minds** that doesn't give strength to interjecting failure when there's no apparent reason why we should fail, **success will become a part of our every action.**

There is a key to success that is studied in many of the other chapters throughout this book that involves the concept of creating habits, because once a habit is developed, it's easier to make that practice a part of our life. As we eliminate what I like to call the *failure response syndrome,* the pressure created from competition will disappear. As a matter of fact, we've all seen those individuals who react better under pressure, and perform to even greater lengths when there is competition. That is because those individuals still relate to the "I dare you" level that we spoke of earlier. They feel that someone is questioning whether or not they can perform to a certain level. They are bound and determined to demolish and stop such ideas so that there is little doubt in the future. Another reason why many individuals routinely perform to a good level, but excel when the pressure of competition has been presented comes from the feeling of being *center stage* or on exhibit—and don't we all want to be noticed? Doesn't this individual say, *"Yeah, I've been doing fine at what I'm doing, but now everybody's noticing, so look out world"*? Well, why can't we use that attitude to our advantage? Why is it that we take the opposite approach? *"Everyone's* looking now and I don't like the pressure of everyone staring at what I'm doing. Why are they questioning what I'm doing? Why are they looking at what I'm doing? Why is it important at all? End result: *failure.*

The fact is they are looking, and whether they're waiting for you to fail or succeed has no bearing on the outcome. Only we control the outcome. One of the best ways of eliminating that pressure is to eliminate those ominous eyes that we have created in our mind that watch every action. Instead, we have to concentrate on the things that we do well and what makes it possible to succeed. We have to *taste, smell,* and *feel* success, not failure. It's like the age-old devil whispering in one ear and the angel in the other. We have a choice to submit to what's wrong or rejoice in what's right. We must forget (as mentioned before) the spectators or the ever-widened eyes. We should see them cheering or applauding—looking with admiration at the result of success we have attained. So the next time you feel a little pressure or doubt, try to remember a little verse from the Irish poet Goldsmith:

"Our greatest glory consists not in never failing, but in rising every time we fall."

10

Success Suggestions

Success Suggestions for the Athlete

1. Try to avoid excuses for mistakes—learn from them.

2. Don't let people who are going nowhere take you with them.

3. Read every day.

4. Find worthwhile figureheads. Learn the common denominators to their success (be a sponge).

5. Have a good sense of humor.

6. Learn to like workouts.

7. Learn to love people, to get along with people.

8. Measure your progress, every day, week, month, year, etc., but practice persistence with patience.

9. Be loyal to your sport, cause, and other working counterparts.

10. Avoid unfair criticisms or backstabbing practices.

11. Establish principles, but be flexible enough to change.

12. Be an idealist and a realist, the two are not mutually exclusive.

13. Avoid too much TV—it is a waste of time.

14. Get a good hobby or personal activity. Be well-rounded.

15. Support an association, institution, organization, etc.

16. Ignore ignorance; it is catching.

17. Be on time, and clock conscious. Timing and intensity are essential to improving in your sport.

18. Make worthwhile goals (career and personal).

19. Work toward Reaching Your Goals. Goals should be made with careful thought. Someone once said, "Goals should be within one's touch, but not within one's grasp."

20. Organize ideas, systems. Work smart, be scientific, avoid wasted energy.

21. Reward yourself for achievements, punish yourself or make sacrifices for poor performances.

22. Be a good listener.

23. Help others; teachers gain more from the teaching experience than do the students.

24. Refuel your motivation. Be enthusiastic, stay young.

25. Always be a pro.

26. Be as good or better than what you think you are.

27. Be thankful for everything and remember, if you have problems, someone always has it worse.

Part III
The Arts

In all fields, but especially the Arts, press is integral to overall success. Here are copies of some articles published over the years.

Some Reviews of Certo's Novel
The Valor Of Francesco D'Amini

"...Certainly well written..."

—Christopher Leach
Editor in Chief
New Jersey Monthly

"...Poignantly illustrated..."

—Kathleen Longo
The Daily Journal

"...Dominic Certo impresses me even more with the feelings put forth in his new book. An excellent poet, an even better novel writer. His new book is an in depth look into one man's soul. It is moving, packed with feeling and emotion. Mr. Certo states on page 139 'My words have become useless, like the poetry within me.' (Not true) for his words and poetry are felt to the fullest extent."

—Joanne Amadeo
Editor in Chief
Vega Magazine

Winner of Vega's Writer Award For Prose-1979
Publisher's Nominee-1980 American Book Award (New Novels)

The author at 18 in Vietnam

Certo receiving a combat action award and Vietnamese Cross of Gallantry with
Bronze Star while in I Corps-Vietnam (age 19).

CERTO'S KNIGHTING & INVESTITURE, TO THE ORDER OF SAINT JOHN OF RUSSIA, BY HIS EXCELLENCY, COUNT NICHOLAS A BOBRINSKOY, GREAT-GREAT-GREAT GRANDSON OF EMPRESS CATHERINE THE GREAT, AT THE RUSSIAN CATHEDRAL OF THE HOLY VIRGIN.

11

The Arts

Michelangelo, Vermeer, Hemingway, Dickens, Caruso, Streisand, Frost, and Browning are all great people, all with varied interests, and are *all great artists!* What passion gives these people the great gift to create? What luck of fate allowed their celebration when the world is filled with wonderful artists? Is there a tried formula? Well, there is and it can be applied to almost any individual. The degree of inherent talent cannot be transferred, but the guidelines for using and improving what you have can be perfected and ultimately bring you success. One thing you must understand before we go any farther: Much of what I outline, along with the contributions shared from those herein, is relative to each area, business and sports as well. Success in any endeavor depends upon a tried method that obtains results. Let's look at them in order:

First, establish short-range, mid-range, and long-range goals with the focus on the short-range, but the fuel for thought coming from the long-range goals. Then develop a *logical,* researched, and no nonsense road map that will take you to where you're going.

Next, study it, memorize it, internalize it. Make it your own. Let it fit like a tailored suit. Believe in it! *It's Your Baby and Your Plan!* Write it down, keep it in the book you read, the car you drive or by the bed where you sleep. When it becomes part of the decor and less noticeable, change the paper or the wording. *Re-Internalize It!* (To coin a new word?)

Now that you have goals and a plan, make sure that that goal or plan includes *knowledge!* You must be an expert (not a technician). You must be an expert in the necessities of what carries you to the top. For instance in writing, knowing that your plot must always have the reader engrossed is more important than a debate over using a comma or a semicolon. Both are important, but you need the best understanding of the engine before you rewire the car.

Keep track of your progress. Reward your successes and understand your mistakes but don't let them create a neurosis. The world is full of unsuccessful people who are good at what they do and the world is also full of neurotics. Help your progress along with improvements to your road map as you discover better methods and new innovations. Ask questions of those who have traveled the way you are attempting—and succeeded.

Always remember that in the Arts there are two measures for evaluating the art (to some degree), the artist and the masses. Do not create for the masses but to the masses. Let me explain. In 1976, I wrote my first novel, which, in the purest sense of the words, was my heart, mind and soul put to paper. It was created from deep within and I wanted to impart that subjectivity to everyone. I had to let people feel my feelings, see what I had seen and share with them a profound experience. I couldn't accomplish that if my attitude was independent of concern for the reader. My novel would have become a drifting piece of prose that served little purpose except to indulge and sublimate the artist in me. Never become commercially ruled in your creativity, for that will make you but another thread in the fiber—not the cloth itself. Create, be intense, be profound, express and reach, but remember the masses. They will help your expression.

Never be overwhelmed by the "big picture." Always break it down into smaller components. A book is but pages and chapters, a painting but strokes of a brush, a sculpture but chips off stone. Work every day so that your creativity and art become your work. Be happy you have chosen your life's work, and that you and you alone are responsible for it. Be content in its beauty. Your creation will live on long after your life's spent. You have shared a piece of your soul and embraced your fellow man. You, my friend, are the spirit of humanity!

Tony DeNonno

(Producer, Writer, Director & Songwriter)
Brooklyn, New York

Filmmaker Tony DeNonno has Produced, Written & Directed more than fifty award-winning documentary films for American and world audiences. He has received numerous "Outstanding Film of the Year" awards at the American, New York, London, Los Angeles, Australian, and San Francisco Film Festivals.

Tony DeNonno's documentary films honor the values, traditions and diversity of America and are in the permanent collection of the Museum of Modern Art, alongside directors Martin Scorsese and Woody Allen, etc.

In more than two dozen TV productions, Tony DeNonno has celebrated the traditions, values, and vast contributions New Yorkers of all backgrounds have made to the fabric of America and the world. Many are considered "timeless classics," which are continually being broadcast on TV and Cable Stations worldwide—and have been acquired by Universities, Schools, Museums, Libraries and Cultural Organizations across North America and around the world. His films have been broadcast on almost every major American television network: ABC, NBC, CBS, Fox, HBO, PBS, USA, Showtime and on TV Stations worldwide.

He has been praised by Janet Maslin of the New York Times *for his "…deft and impressive filmmaking." And for being "intuitively aware of the subject's uniqueness, individuality and significance to society." He has also Produced and/or Directed more than twenty-five Television Commercials and Public Service Announcements. Mr. DeNonno has directed three Off-Broadway Plays and has written two plays as well. A Songwriter and member of ASCAP, DeNonno has composed and/or co-written the musical score for more than fifteen Documentary Films. He has written both the Music & Lyrics to more than two-dozen pop songs.*

Since 9/11 after witnessing the towers burn and losing four friends, he has written an average of two compositions-songs a month, which have evolved into the heart of an original Broadway musical he is writing entitled: "To Love Divine." It is a love story of betrayal, survival, and redemption in the aftermath of 9/11. The Flatbush Tompkins Gospel Choir premiered the play's title song, "To Love Divine" in May 2002.

Between 1970 and 1993 award-winning TV producer-writer-director Tony DeNonno worked as a freelance photographer/photojournalist. In photographing some of the greatest legends of the entertainment industry, both behind the scenes and in performance, Tony amassed an impressive collection of more than 20,000 photo-

graphs, some of which have been featured in Time, Newsweek, People, Vogue *and* Rolling Stone. *From Frank Sinatra and Muddy Waters to John Lennon and Bob Dylan; from Cary Grant and Bill Cosby to Mick Jagger, Richard Prior and Aretha Franklin; from Elvis to Muhammad Ali and Bette Midler; from Ella Fitzgerald and Lena Horne to Barbra Streisand and Marvin Gaye; from Jackie Kennedy Onassis to Tina Turner and Rod Stewart; from Andy Warhol and Alan Ginsberg to Ray Charles, The Who and Frank Zappa—Tony DeNonno's photographs capture the essence of this golden era in entertainment history. He was the exclusive photographer for Eric Clapton's 1974 Tour of America and also took photographs at the legendary Bangladesh Concert, Secretariat's Triple Crown Victory at the Belmont Stakes and the New York Knicks World Championship in 1970.*

Whether it is film, video, drama, photographs and song, Tony DeNonno is a story-teller who continually aspires to "reveal human truths and moments in a person's life—and in so doing, captures a brief story of feeling, spirit and emotion that hopefully touches a chord in all of us."

Tony DeNonno offers the following Success Tips:

More than thirty years ago, at the beginning of my career, in order to supplement my vision as a filmmaker, I was a freelance photojournalist writing for a publication called *Military Life* serving our Armed Forces worldwide. The opening line of a feature article I wrote about a young contender working his way up to the Golden Gloves championship and stills resonates with me as I begin reflecting on success. "Losers are winners with a flaw and in boxing there is no exception." This young boxer lost the championship bout because, for a split second, he let his guard down, lost his focus and ultimately his sense of himself, his power and strength. So for me the most profound teacher about success in my life is through the gateway of my failures, then learning about them and acting upon them proactively.

Always listening. As I reflect on the successes in my life, it is when I was lying flat on my back on the canvas of life I truly learned the lessons for success. For whenever I let my guard down and put my desire for money, to prove a point or my self-worth and letting frustration, rage, or desperation rule me, it guaranteed failure.

Doing my homework. Whenever I did my homework, discovering the mission, essence of my potential clients or employer and finding, planning and facilitating a common ground where a meeting of the minds, and more importantly a meeting of the hearts truly took place then success was guaranteed.

Don't beat yourself up. If it is not meant to be it is not meant to be, no matter how perfect you are for the position, or how illogical, unfair, difficult and unjust life is at times. The true meaning of success is taking care of your self, forgiving and ultimately loving yourself be it shortcomings and all. Cry the cries, scream the screams at home, alone or with your therapist and don't take them to the doorstep of your potential employer, client or especially at someone in your family.

Honor your heart. Find your own voice in the world. Find what nurtures, protects and celebrates you. Love and/or make peace with what you do. Find your own purpose in the world, if not in your workplace, in your home and or community. Don't make your job the end all. Savor the things that nurture and love you.

Transporting People with passion. I consider myself a storyteller. Whether I am producing a documentary film, a promotional film for a cultural institution, school or corporation, writing a screenplay, or a song my goal is always to touch a chord in people of all ages. I always aspire to enlighten, guide and transport them into a life a place, a story, a melody that is compelling, moment by moment; and hopefully, entertaining, heartwarming and enlightening as well.

Feeling blessed. I feel blessed with the gifts that God has given me. I admire my Italian Ancestors, whose work ethic, devotion, and enduring sacrifice to their family's future is unquestionable. Americans live to work but Italians work to live. They truly savor and celebrate life. I abide with this philosophy everyday and do my utmost to continuously try to savor the moments in my daily work and home life. My production cast, crews, editors, interns, production assistants, and I, always celebrate our little victories and accomplishments sometimes during the course of a day.

Teamwork and Togetherness. I try to guide, challenge and inspire myself and everyone who works with me to set a goal for the day and to complete at least one task a hand. It is an essential ingredient of success. During the course of a day, I always encourage everyone individually as well as collectively to take breaks for it enhances professional excellence and achievement in the work place. Sharing a fine meal, savoring a sweet desert, taking a mid-day walk or some fine wine at the end of the day; is part of our working environment. The demands and intensity of creating art can be incredible. Therefore taking a moment to celebrate the completion of a scene, a song, a grant proposal, or a sale is a must for me. A walk in the park is a wonderful antidote to the intense pressure, and unrelenting deadlines inherent in the entertainment industry and perhaps all fields of endeavor in the 21st Century. To paraphrase Beethoven, "It's not the music, but the 'space' between the music that really counts." Creativity, inspiration and productivity soars whenever you take a break, let things breathe and especially when you honor and paying homage to completing what you set out to complete—by resting on your laurels both individually and collectively. Finally I always give a special thanks to each and everyone who supports and enhances my vision by giving them recognition at the end for a job well done.

Recognizing your True Voice in the World. At the heart of what I do as a filmmaker, songwriter, and director is to mine the essence and core of the individual(s) I am focusing upon, and reveal something about him or her, which touches a chord in all of us. I see myself as a storyteller and I love to shine my filmmaker's eye on the often unspoken and unrecognized "Salt of the Earth" individuals of this world—whose daily lives I feel are sublime and whose essence, heart, soul, and wisdom for living are truly inspirational to us all. I feel blessed that my documentary films evolved into timeless classics and are continually being broadcast and showcased at universities, museums, and libraries around the world. I also appreciate the gift and opportunity to celebrate the heritage, values, and traditions of people of all cultures and creeds in our great nation and especially the chance to honor the indelible contributions individuals of Italian descent have make to the fabric of America and the world.

Never Giving Up and Letting it Breathe. My last nationally broadcast PBS Network documentary "Heaven Touches Brooklyn in July" was eighteen years in the making and lovingly edited from over 140 hours of film footage. Presently I am working on a documentary I began in 1996 entitled "A Century of Laughter, Heart and Song." During the course of making both of the films over the last decade I had to put them aside, let them rest for months and sometimes years at a time. Sometimes it was to raise the essential funds to take the project to the next phase. On both productions, they remained untouched for up to three years but I never abandon my passionate belief and dream to complete them one day. I never gave up for I felt right from the beginning that these are story that must be told.

Seek out mentors, supporters, people who can talk straight with you. Both of my grandfathers died before I was born. My father, like most fathers of his generation was absentee, so I always sought out mentors—men and women who have enhanced the quality and touched every phase of my filmmaking, screenplay and songwriting, theatrical writing directing, and photographic career with their wisdom, straight talking insight and feedback.

Keeping your faith and beliefs alive. In April of 2005, I lost faith, my optimistic spirit, was at the lowest of lows. Physically, spiritually, and psychologically, I was angry frustrated and at the point of giving it all up. Then my greatest dream of my life was realized. Today at 59 years old, I finally met my soul mate. I am getting married and becoming a father, too. When all hope is gone, your dreams can still endure and manifest in reality even when all hope is gone. Everything in its time. Have patience to wait.

I never gave up my dream. I feel that I can shine my filmmaker's eye on anyone in the world no matter what age, race, or creed and I know in telling their story, it will have resonance and substance for us all. I realize everything has a place and time. When I create a song, I continually seek out people of all ages to guide and inspire me and provide me with straight talk about the work I am creating.

I believe that all the wisdom of the world, future inventions, cures and dreams of creation, peace of mind and prosperity is in each and every one of us. All we have to believe, respect nurture and recognize our own gifts and wisdom for living and making a living.

I wrote an upbeat swing style dance song entitled "Listen to Your Soul." One verse proclaims Listen to Your Soul it's the force from which we flow, it's the path connecting all of us, it's the grace of growing old.

Find you path and travel down it with reckless abandon with all your heart, passion and soul.

We humans are fallible. I try my best not to beat myself. Rejection is a large part of the entertainment industry. So I continually try to move forward and not enable anyone or thing to be a knockout punch that sends me crashing to the canvas, unconsciously lost without a conscience or a compass. Recognize that in so doing you are undermining yourself and causing self-inflicted wounds that sap your energy, spirit and ability to succeed. Know also when to bite your tongue, and own up to your mistake and don't blame it on others or you will be fated to repeat it over and over again.

Don't be afraid of your vulnerability. Share it to those you trust and love. It takes a conscious, responsible and honest way of reaching out again…owning your mistakes and/flaws sometimes with a sincere apology (to yourself first and foremost). Take your time, catch your breath before communicating and finding a common ground where your needs and desires meet those of your clients, your friends, and loved ones. I am not afraid of revealing my vulnerability and my needs.

Love Learning like a Wide-Eyed Child. I love learning. Throughout my career, I have always loved learning about an individual area of study and presenting it to the world as a wondrous story. I am able to do this because I am not afraid to ask questions, to admit I don't know, and quest and accumulation of knowledge gives me the ability to enchant the wide-eyed children of all ages around the world with a story that meets their yearnings of the wonders of life.

Find your smile. Be at home with who you are and learn to forgive yourself. Give yourself a little gift of love each day, a reward, a breather, a break. For me it is holding and being held, a piece of dark chocolate, a swim in the ocean, savoring a dinner, a glass of wine, a dinner with the people I love. Life is made of moments and even a simple baseball catch with your dad or moment with your mom can resonate forever as priceless and unforgettable.

Own your power, your strength. Discover the way(s) you fit or have a common ground with a client or fit within a particular company by researching everything you can about them, truly hearing them in your meetings—and then responding to them from the depth of your compassion, understanding ability to meet or support their needs. Rest assured that time and again this devotion will always guarantee success. It will enable you to flow in a natural rhythm and in harmony with them and create a meeting of the minds that enhance all future endeavors.

Completing and competing in the face of adversity. Keep your faith alive. Never give up reaching with your hands outstretched trying to grasp the golden ring of life...even if they are torn to shreds. Survival is also essential and learning to hear, mine and know how to nurture and protect yourself on the journey to success, is essential. Life is brutal at times, fraught with tragedy, danger, and destruction and so all of sail on the River Styx experience, the Dante Alighieri's Ninth Circle of Hell—but its take to courage to go on and a willingness to change in order to climb out of the depths of Hell or fly out of it like the Phoenix. Turn your pain your loss, your rage, your self-loathing into action. Change comes from recognition and devotion to protecting yourself, mostly from yourself. Reaching out to the world, to individuals for the life-saving ingredients that can guide, challenge provoke and inspire you during the rough seas toward success in life are some of the greatest gifts of healing and achievement.

Life is but a dream. I know I always succeed when I am not trying to push the river...but instead by finding a way to win others by discovering my own voice and rhythm of truth that flows in natural harmony and motion with the partners I am inviting or who are inviting me to dance. So together we can sway together with a shared vision for the company and its future. What drives me is not monetary gain, revenge or the thirst for success, but truly a desire to soothe a soul, touch a heart, of children of all ages, backgrounds and beliefs around the world. I always say and firmly believe: "It's not a world of perfection but a world of completion." I know I am a storyteller always trying to connect with and share the golden bread, the glory of a life that is truly sublime, that alights the soul, and is a the true gift of our humanity. Wishing you rousing success that is your birthright and at the heart of you and me.

Karen Kristine Clarke

(Professional Photographer)
Long Island, New York

Karen is one of the leading sports photographers in the country. Her work has appeared in Sports Illustrated, Shape, Muscle & Fitness, Flex, Muscle Training Illustrated, Iron Man Magazine *and several others. Her excellent action photos have been used by every major TV network and in several "prime time shows." Her cat pic-*

tures are award-winning and her photography talents extend to other areas and media, including Baby Talk Magazine, Cat Fancy, *and* Recreation LIFE. *Her photos have also appeared in newspapers all over the country, including the* Daily News, New York Post, Washington Post, Los Angeles Times *and several others. Much of her work is featured in this text.*

Recently her poster work was shown in a Toyota commercial segment where weightlifters were used as well as promotional events for Caesar's Palace, the Playboy Club and Resorts International. Karen is partners with Wayne DeMilia in Physique Productions and helps coordinate and manage several bodybuilding events he promotes. She is a graduate of Manhattan Community College with a degree in Physical Education. Her background in sports helped contribute to her unique ability to capture the look of a champion. Karen herself was a member of swimming, diving and softball teams all through her school years and in 1971 was named Female Athlete of the Year. Here are her thoughts and suggestions:

"There are times when you study and work for one field and by the time you reach your best potential, the 'Field' has passed you by—either by progression of a rapid pace or the employment fizzle of a chosen field. Most good careers demand highly qualified people with many years of experience. Which you can't develop if no one will employ you. If you can branch out to other fields as I did—you will stand a real chance to accomplish something of meaning for yourself.

I had an advantage—my best friend, Wayne DeMilia supported me in every way a best friend could. I did get depressed after going to college to become a Recreation/Physical Ed teacher, only to find out that there was an overflow of teachers and no jobs in sight. Then being employed by NYC and being let go when all programs were cancelled because the City went broke was a setback, too. Two thousand people lost their jobs in 1977, but I was doing photography at the time and had a chance to pursue that career. It has been very kind to me.

Always try your talents in other areas just to test the water and get a feel for your own abilities, you may be surprised."

Alan J. Paul

(Author—Editor)

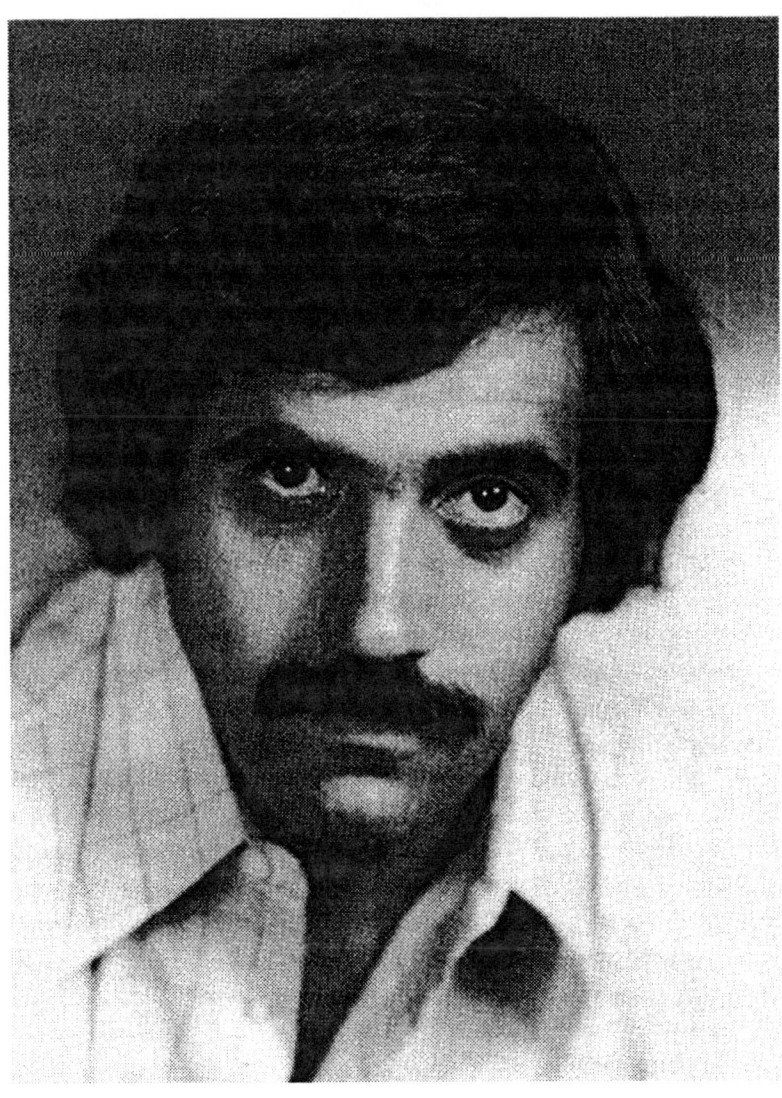

Graduate of Rutgers University 1971 (B.A. Journalism)
Served as special consultant to the Corporation for Public Broadcasters. *Always a freelance writer while acting as a managing editor for several national sports magazines. His articles and interviews have appeared in* US, Neve Revue, New Body *and others.*
Alan wrote the book John The COP *about Brooklyn, New York policeman and karate master, John Maniel.*

Success is a matter of degrees, and only the individual can know whether the success in life he has experienced is that which he has sought and strived for. To the recent journalism school graduate, for example, a position on the staff of a major newspaper or magazine might be the object of his fantasies. While to the veteran reporter/journalist who really wants to be a novelist, his job is at best a means to an end. But each of us must have a goal—rather a series of goals, and the determination to realize them.

No one ever became a success without a certain amount of talent, in whatever field. But often it is not the person with the most talent who succeeds. More likely, it is the overachievers of this world—the people who, in lieu of absolute ability are blessed with tenacity of purpose and strong self-confidence—who succeed, perhaps even beyond their own expectations.

Having a thick skin is a definite plus since, in journalism and the arts in particular, learning to deal with an avalanche of rejection is imperative. If one can overcome waves of rejection and persevere with ego relatively intact, the chances of eventual success are greatly improved. If you happen to be one who discourages easily, you will probably entertain success only in your dreams. While our dreams are important, reality can be much more satisfying.

There are many times when you will falter in your quest; I certainly have, and will no doubt continue to do so. Each time I do, I am reminded of a scene from the movie, "Little Big Man," starring Dustin Hoffman. In the film, the Hoffman character accompanies his ancient Indian mentor to the place where the old chief/magician plans to give up his soul to The Creator. He lays down to die. After some long moments, he opens his eyes and sits up. Hoffman approaches him, saying something like, "Grandfather, what happened? You didn't die!"

"Well, my son," replies the old man, resigned. "Sometimes the magic works...and sometimes it doesn't."

The key to success is getting your personal magic working as often as possible.

Lori Goldman Ames

(Editor-Publicist)
Long Island, New York

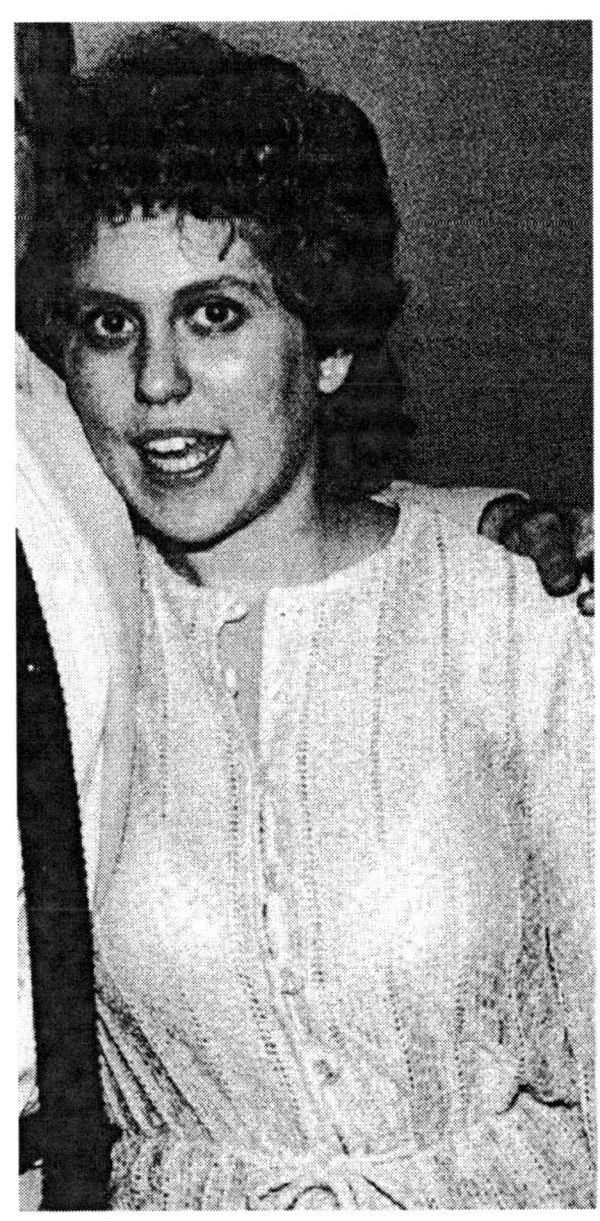

Lori is the Director of Client Services at Jane Wessman Public Relations, *928 Broadway, New York City, New York 10010. She is the former editor of* Manor Books *Park Avenue, New York, and has her Bachelors Degree in advertising and journalism. Lori is well-known in New York City and throughout the country for her energetic personality and sincere concern for the authors (artists) she represents. Her duties include publicity, promotional tours and advertising for several prominent authors and celebrated artists. Here are some important points she makes:*

"Every artist must consider what happens to a book, painting or sculpture after it is completed. In order to be appreciated by the masses it must be promoted. If an artist can gear his or her talents and personality to reach out, their chances of success are far greater, and if the artist is reading this piece, isn't that what they're after?

I find my job so much easier if the creator of a piece empathizes with the challenging job I have of getting the author and work celebrated. The competition is great, everybody wants a piece of the action. So when we work hand-in-hand the results come faster and with better success.

But first, the work must be good. Don't be too slanted in your views so that it's evident. Be a little objective, you're looking for mass appeal so step away from time to time and look at your work.

I had the opportunity to work with Dom Certo on his first book. Our editors felt the book was great and so did the reviewers but we had the task of getting acceptance for a first time novelist. Because he worked with us the whole ordeal went a lot smother. Keep that in mind when working toward release and market penetration.

To sum it up, be conscientious, thorough, and objective. Pick a good agent, publisher and publicity firm and you'll go far."

Beth J. Schenerman

(Freelance Journalist & Author)
Brooklyn, New York

Beth has appeared in publications all over the country. Her work can be found in: the New York Times, Boxing World, The Newark Star Ledger, The New Tri- bune, New Jersey Monthly, The Independent, Programmers Exchange Magazine *and many others. She is a graduate of Douglass College with a B.A. in English. At school she was a member of the Dean's List on several occasions and won several essay awards in both fiction and non-fiction. Beth studied creative writing with the cele-*

brated sportswriter Barbara Long. She worked as a reporter for the Rutgers Targum, The Bayshore Independent *and* The Newark Star Ledger. *Currently she is a consultant and administrator for the Israeli Consulate on Mission to the United Nations while she completes her new book.*

Herewith, her feelings on being a writer:

I must admit I know a couple of very good techniques for putting my writing across to editors. I didn't learn them at Douglass College where I put in four years as just another English major, showing up for classes on those rare occasions when my boyfriend and I were fighting or he had to go to work and I had nothing else to do. When I could get myself to sit still long enough to write something that turned out so pure and beautiful that I didn't know whether to cry or sleep for the next two weeks in simple exhaustion, I fell back on early childhood training and did neither. I'm not ashamed to say I needed cheerleaders when I did something I was proud of and my Mom and Pop could usually be relied upon to sit still and listen to me read my entire Work of Art, even if it took an hour or two, even if my mother dozed on and off as the clock in their bedroom ticked past four o'clock in the morning. This gave me a lot of confidence. My parents were so desperate to sleep that they would say anything to encourage me to leave them. They told me I was the Greatest Writer In The World and my subject matter was The Most Interesting Thing They Had Ever Heard In Their Lives. Can you imagine how much guts and chutzpah I had when, a couple hours later, I started calling up editors to sell my story? I talked to those guys like I talked to my grandparents (whom I also called) because I knew I had something really terrific here and how could they not want to know about it? If they didn't I kvetched, whined and nagged and once, I even dropped in on the Jersey Editor in the *New York Times* newsroom, sat down at an empty desk and munched on apples and other assorted fruit I brought in my pocketbook until he found time to read my story. Of course it got published. The main thing was getting him to read it. I'm not a teacher, but I don't think anyone can teach writing anyway. You can pick up some hints and tips on improving your writing from reading books and talking to other writers, but you have got to have what it takes to begin with, and that comes from somewhere deep down inside."

Ben Weider, CM.

(Author—Historian—Statesman & Businessman)

Author of several books, including his new bestseller and blockbuster success The Murder of Napoleon *by Congdon & Lattes (distributed by St. Martin's Press). Jack Nicholson has purchased the movie rights and has hired Bo Goodman (the person who wrote the scenario for* One Flew Over The Cuckoo's Nest *for the film. Jack Nicholson intends to play the lead role of Napoleon. The book has been published in condensed form in* Readers Digest *and 17 foreign translations were made, covering 31 million copies.* Encyclopedia Britannica *will be including information about the death of Napoleon and refer to the book in their next edition. The book has been published in the following languages: English, French, Spanish, Italian, German, Swedish, Japanese and Portuguese. Ben is a collector of Napoleonic memorabilia—his new Napoleon piece was featured on the cover of* History Book Club Review *(April 1982) and given a full page in* Newsweek. *He is president of the IFBB (International Federation of Bodybuilders), member of the Order of Canada, faculty teacher of the U.S. Sports Academy, and research contributor to the Olympic Committees. Ben has received the* Queen's Silver Jubilee Medal. *He has 36 years of experience in sports, business, the arts, and has traveled over 90 countries. His fitness business concern is one of the largest in the world. He has scheduled two new books for release in the coming year:* Fit For Life *(general fitness for all ages) and* Judgment on Napoleon *(the Emperor's contributions to humanity and an overall review of the man).*

Ben is also shown on the front cover.

150 YEARS LATER, MODERN FORENSIC MEDICINE
DISCOVERS ONE OF HISTORY'S GREATEST CRIMES,
THE MURDER OF NAPOLEON
BY BEN WEIDER &
DAVID HAPGOOD

B. Weider Published Congdon & Lattes, Distributed by St. Martin's
Press.

Note from the Author: Ben Weider is more than the achievements and credentials he has earned. He has always been a gentleman and humanitarian. He epitomizes the utmost integrity in all he does. When asked to help in this journal and give insight to his success and guidelines for the struggling artist, businessman or athlete, he made every effort to genuinely contribute his feelings. Herewith are his commentaries:

Certo: Ben, what do you think was your biggest inspiration to write *The Murder of Napoleon?*

Ben: Well I believe that Napoleon was a great man. I think he lived actually before his time because his dreams of creating a United States of Europe is exactly what we are trying to do now, to have a European congress. He believed that there should be one people, no borders, one congress, one type of currency and one law for everybody, so everybody would be equal. That was his main dream, but, that dream was created during the feudal system when kings ran everything and did not care very much for democracy and freedom and equality so he was a little bit ahead of his time. I admired him because of his ability to achieve things against all odds and the achievement was always based on the freedom and equality of people regardless of who they were: Protestants, Catholics, Jews, any nationality or any religion.

Certo: That's an interesting point. What do you think came first, your interest in the writing or your interest in the subject?

Ben: Interest in the subject. I had no idea of doing the book whatsoever but, because I did grow to admire his achievements and admired the man, his last wish was that the cause of his death be known and I think that I and Dr. Forshufvud of Sweden have fulfilled his last dying wish.

Certo: Well, the book is a marvelous success. Did you expect it to have this kind of appeal?

Ben: I knew it would be popular to a point because it's still a history book you see and you know history books don't become best sellers. Now the *Murder of Napoleon* is number two on the best sellers list in Canada, it's sold over 110,000 hard cover books and is now in paperback done by Berkeley. Jack Nicholson has bought the rights to make a movie and then again the *Encyclopedia Britannica* has written me a letter and told me they are going to revise their section on Napoleon to include this part about his life and poisoning on St. Helena. So these are the major achievements. Another major achievement is *Readers Digest* selected my book. You see, there are, I think, 45 to 50,000 different titles published in the U.S.A. every year. *Readers Digest* picks 12 of them for their book sections because they only have 12 editions a year. For them to pick my book to review as a book section is a major achievement; also, they have 17 foreign editions with 31 million readers and it's up to the foreign editors to decide if they want to re-publish the book as selected by the American head office or they can select local books as they wish, yet every one of the 17 foreign editions picked up the American review of my book.

Certo: That's fantastic.

Ben: Thank you! It was read by 31 million people.

Certo: What do you feel are the most necessary ingredients to a successful artist or any struggling artist who is approaching such a project?

Ben: I think, first of all they have to have an interesting subject, and second of all, they have to put themselves in the shoes of the reader. They've got to open the book with a paragraph that is riveting. A paragraph that will grasp their imagination and prevent them from putting the book down. If they don't do that on the first page they have a good chance of having lost the reader.

Certo: You have a lot of other responsibilities, including the IFBB and your business and so forth. How often did you work on your book?

Ben: On and off it took at least 15 years. This includes the testing and various trips I had to make to meet with Forshufvud to compare notes and so forth. We have a very critical problem. History has already established itself that Napoleon had died from some other source and the most popular source of the death was cancer of the stomach. Now, if we had the slightest flaw in our thesis we knew we would be crucified by historians that have already accepted the fact that Napoleon was poisoned, died of cancer and would be hard for them to go back on what they believed because it would be harmful to their reputation. Especially the French historians. So we have to be extremely careful that all our testing would be beyond reproach and that is exactly what has happened. Not one toxicologist or not one medical person who has any knowledge of toxicology opposed the thesis which was confirmed by nuclear science.

Certo: It's amazing that something like this kind of a breakthrough wasn't done sooner.

Ben: Yes. Because the evidence was flagrant basically, how does somebody die of stomach cancer without manifesting its symptoms? If you have a disease you have to have some symptoms of the specific disease. Napoleon had no symptoms of stomach cancer. How did they explain Napoleon being fat if we accept the thesis he was suffering from stomach cancer and he suffered from these symptoms for a period of almost five years? How come he still remained fat? And nobody could live five years without being treated properly in the modern sense and live with stomach cancer. It's one of the most wasting of the diseases. So how could he suffer for five years with stomach cancer and still remain fat? And finally, what's the explanation of those high levels of arsenic that were found in his hair. There has to be a reason. There is only one way they could have got it into his body—two ways. Either he took the arsenic himself because he wanted to commit suicide, or somebody fed it to him. Otherwise there's no way that so much arsenic can get into his hair.

Certo: Let me ask you this. Your schedule is so active and busy now, most things are prearranged to an extent. Did you have to establish a great deal of goals in the earlier days to meet the kind of success you met with?

Ben: You mean the goals for my success in bodybuilding or my business?

Certo: Well, I would say mostly as a writer, but in general—success in general. I guess you had to set some sort of goals, didn't you?

Ben: Yes. By order and priority my main goal was to establish a source of revenue that I can feel secure with so this would enable me to do things that I considered my hobby or cultural interests. My main goal was to establish my business and make sure it was on solid ground, that our name would be known the world over and be a demand for the products so I didn't let anything deter me from that. My years between 1946 and 1964 were dedicated mainly to the development of the Weider name throughout the world and the creation of a business rooted in solid ground.

Certo: You certainly do a good job businesswise, also. Your name is widely known and a true compliment to your success in that arena. What is your next literary project? Do you have another one in mind?

Ben: Well, there's two. I've written another book called *Judgment On Napoleon.* It's an overall book depicting all his contributions to humanity while he was the emperor of the French. An overall view of Napoleon as a man. And then there's another book called *Fit for Life.* It's a book describing all of my ideas on health and fitness, because I strongly believe that a person does not have to age before his time. I believe a person who's 50 should be as energetic as a person who's 25. I believe a person who's 70 can still be very energetic like he was at 45 or 50. There is no reason why a person of 70 should have to be confined to a bed or confined to home or hobble along. I believe a person 70 can still be energetic, can swim, jog, dance and go to the movies, theaters and so forth and still enjoy life. I believe that there is a slowing down of the aging processes through fitness and proper nutrition and food supplementation.

Certo: Sounds like you're headed for the best seller list again.

Ben: Well, I'm working very hard on that book. That'll be the expression of everything I believe in.

Certo: Both books are interesting to me, particularly the book on Napoleon's contribution. I've always been a big fan of Napoleon and I've read some of his works, one of the most recent ones was Kronin's piece, but that goes back a few years. Let me ask you this, Ben, do you come from an artistic family?

Ben: No. Not really.

Certo: It's not a product of the genes?

Ben: No, it's something that I just must have inbred in me which was brought out during my numerous travels. Since 1946, I've been to over 90 countries and this is in all the continents of the world, met all types of people from kings to workers, truck drivers, whatever and I've always had contact and respect with everybody on every level. I don't have any more respect for a king than I do for a truck driver. Everything depends on his own ability to communicate and this opened broad avenues of culture.

Certo: Let me ask you a couple of last questions. Did you experience many rejections and obstacles when you started the project? For example, the assassination at St. Helena which was originally part of this project?

Gen: The only opposition I experienced was with a certain society in France because I'm a member of their executive and they represent a group of French historians who have already established, and are known for the fact that they accepted the thesis of Napoleon dying of cancer and would be highly embarrassing to them to have scientific proof that he died of something else. I keep telling them that an historian's duty is not to protect theses or protect history. An historian's duty is to look for the truth and tell the truth no matter what and no matter whom it affects. They practically threatened me that if I would go ahead with this book and have it published that they would do everything within their power to ridicule the book and ridicule the thesis and try to have me humiliated.

Certo: Did they do much, or was it mostly a verbal attack?

Ben: No, they contacted the press and prevented me from appearing on TV and having some contact with specific writers, but this did not prevent the book from being a major success in France and, of course, *Readers Digest* in France published the book review so that reached several million people of the popular level. But the weird part is that the majority of these historians privately agreed with the thesis that Napoleon was indeed poisoned through arsenic on some occasion. Privately they did. But publicly they opposed it.

Certo: What about the movie with Nicholson? Do you feel maybe you'll be doing the script or the screen work on it, or will it be an outright sale?

Ben: Well, we made an outright sale to Jack Nicholson the movie star. He in turn hired his good friend Bo Goodman who did the script or the screenplay for "One Flew Over the Cuckoos Nest" and "Chinatown", and I understand that the screenplay is well advanced now and I'll be checking the text to see that the accuracy and historical events are there.

Certo: In closing, what would you tell a struggling artist to aid in their success—particularly the writer or journalist?

Ben: One word only—**Persevere.**

12

The Elephant Story

Some years ago at a guild or business meeting, I heard an "elephant story" that conveys some of the ideas covered in this book. Let me share it with you:

Have you ever given thought to the monstrous and powerful elephant that is a part of every circus? Or given notice to how he is chained within the confines of the tent for public viewing? He walks about in a circle with nothing but a small chain (compared to his size) wrapped around his leg and pinned to the ground. Whenever that huge animal reaches the end of his chain there is a slight jerk and he returns to the area within his allowable circle. The fact is, this great creature could easily pull out the chain and continue on his way exploring and traveling to his heart's content, for after all he did erect the 'big top.' The elephant is the instrument of strength. But he or she is easily discouraged by that short feeble chain. It could even be plastic and hold him. This is a product of conditioning and early training. When the elephant is a baby, it is shackled to a very large object, usually a tree and whenever it feels the urge to escape or fly, it is jerked back by the bonds of its manacles and it learns, painfully at times, that it cannot go beyond its circle of captivity. So, too, is our childhood conditioning. We are told by our parents, many times for our own good, sometimes not, that we can't go here or there, we can't try this or that, we are only so capable or not, which limits us to an unreal understanding of ourselves when we reach adulthood. This might have served some purpose or protection as a child, but as adults we need to escape that infantile meridian. We have all the strength and magnitude of the powerful elephant. We can break those feeble chains, *throw them away and fly!*

Sketch by Kathy McCaffery

Sketch by Kathy McCaffery

13

Go for the Gusto!

What a simple statement. Sounds like a beer commercial, but in this case we're not selling beer. Something far more important—our total happiness and satisfaction. George Bernard Shaw reminds us, "Life is a state of mind" (how true). Once we realize that, the state of mind we choose, whether positive or negative, becomes an ordeal or a joyous experience. I always have a great deal of admiration for those individuals who thoroughly enjoy life. They meet failures and successes with a strong healthy foundation, they *"Live."*

This chapter, though brief, needs to be categorized, because no goal, endeavor, or undertaking can be achieved to any great success for a sustained period of time without a "go for gusto" attitude. How does one Go for Gusto, you ask? For those who see this term vaguely or even those who recognize it, let's examine why it's important. For example: when was the last time you laughed and really enjoyed it? I mean, really laughed so that you felt it way down deep inside, maybe so deep that your cheeks started to hurt or your jaws started to ache, even your eyes started to water? That's *gusto* and I wouldn't replace it for anything in the world. Human beings owe it to themselves to feel that kind of ecstasy. How about the last time you made love and really enjoyed it, so much so that the feeling lingered for days after it was over? That's *gusto!* What about that last big sale where everything went perfectly, true to form and the prospect fell in line with the motivation and solutions you provided? How did you feel? How about when you turned it in? When you didn't compromise your principles and were a true salesperson, what were your feelings? That's *gusto!* Or the time you started a diet, stood on the scale and saw the needle teeter until it finally fell dead center on the desired weight of your goal, how did you feel? That's *gusto!* And the last time your children played with you and made you cry and laugh from love? That's *gusto!* Or when you intercepted that long touchdown pass and ran back 90 yards for your own team's touchdown, how did you feel then? That's *gusto!* So why do we limit ourselves to these isolated moments? Why can't it be more often? The answer is basic. Humans on the whole believe that (this type of) pleasure and enjoyment is an exception, that one cannot consistently sustain highs of fulfillment for any period of time. But we are so wrong, for those individuals who live the longest, share the most and receive the most are those individuals who take pleasure in every aspect of their life.

Do you think it's possible to read a good book with gusto? Certainly! Try creating images in your mind, feeling what the author has presented to you as something important deep within him, even as I'm presenting this material now. Do you think it's possible that one can cook with gusto? Why not? Seeing the value of food and smelling it, tasting it, giving it a different shape or form is exhilarating. If you don't believe it's possible to cook with gusto, visit a French restaurant. How about selling with gusto for the sheer enjoyment of challenge, not just the result? Surely this would make a difference in the attitude of our prospects. How about the manager who manages with feeling and enjoyment, not just because he or she has the title of manager or a raise or promotion? Surely their subordinates could react to that gusto and even instill gusto to their own productivity. All things being equal, two individuals competing, the one with gusto will surpass. Gusto provides more than the immediate gain of enjoyment; it bottom lines to so many other great things. Gusto has character, flavor, finesse, just as showpersonship has similar characteristics. Gusto is that power we sense in people who walk into a room with crowds surrounding them. Gusto is that quality we admire that some people have because they receive more from life than we do.

Gusto can be achieved with very little practice, but once we attempt to invite gusto into our lives, we never let it go. There are some ways of introducing gusto to our lives with little additional effort. The next time you take that walk to the store or your friend's house, rather than drag your feet or question how much better it might be to drive, put a bounce in your walk and a brisk pace to your movements. Feel the air, see the sky, "smell the roses," and a warmth will fill your body like nothing before. As your cheeks get rosy, so will your day. Next time you have that extra workout at the gym, put some extra adrenalin into that pump; smile as your heart picks up the beat and pumps life into your body, taste the oxygen and smell the sweat of your efforts. Feel that you're alive, not just existing. Try to feel your goals next time you contemplate your future—see that new house that you're planning to buy, walk through each room in your mind; smile with a confident satisfaction that the goal is yours. Plan that trip to Bermuda and feel the sun on your face, even though it's raining and the wind is blowing through the trees. See your company's profits as a positive action you will take that will change the course of the negatives you've been expecting for so long. Imagine the celebration dinner as your basketball or football team receives the rewards of an excellent season, while hearing the applause of the spectators who share with you that ecstatic moment. See the sunrise tomorrow morning as you lay in bed and not the darkness, coldness or loneliness of the night. Feel only the God-given beauty of what life has to offer and forget about the sorrow and doubts that creep about like unwanted strangers. Yes, do it with *gusto* and have a beer on me.

NOTES

NOTES

NOTES

NOTES

978-0-595-67929-4
0-595-67929-3

Printed in the United States
66836LVS00004B/61-78

9 780595 679294